Because of Purpose

By Vann Lantz

Helping you unlock your purpose
and achieve the goals
you dream about

Because of Purpose

Copyright © 2020 Vann Lantz.

All rights reserved. No part of this publication may be reproduced, distributed, or transmitted in any form or by any means, including photocopying, recording, or other electronic or mechanical methods, without the prior written permission of the publisher, except in the case of brief quotations embodied in critical reviews and certain other noncommercial uses permitted by copyright law. For permission requests, write to the below address, "Attention: Permissions Coordinator."

ISBN: 978-1-7357865-0-6 (Paperback)

ISBN: 978-1-7357865-1-3 (Hardcover)

ISBN: 978-1-7357865-2-0 (Electronic)

Library of Congress Control Number: 2020917924

Front cover image by Vann Lantz

Front cover design by Vann Lantz and Paul A. Jones

First printing edition 2020

Because of Purpose
PO Box 94
Woodstock, AL 35188

To book Vann for your event, contact:
BOPI@BecauseOfPurpose.com

For more information, go to
https://www.BecauseOfPurpose.com

Dedication

This book is dedicated to my wife, who has been with me for so many years with nothing but loving devotion.

Table of Contents

Introduction	vii
Chapter 1 — What is it All About	3
Chapter 2 — The Starting Point	15
Chapter 3 — How the Mind Works	23
Chapter 4 — Finding what Matters	33
Chapter 5 — Your Dreams	47
Chapter 6 — Mapping it Out	59
Chapter 7 — Walking your Path	79
Chapter 8 — Daily Habits	89
Chapter 9 — Time, Money and More	101
Chapter 10 — An Interview with Paul A Jones	115
Chapter 11 — The Beginning	127

Because of Purpose

Because of Purpose

The steps call for no "hard labor."
They call for no sacrifice.
They do not require one to become
ridiculous or credulous.
To apply them calls for
no great amount of education.

- Napoleon Hill

Chapter 1

What is it All About?

This is Not a Test

I can still remember the feeling, sitting in a classroom waiting for "the other shoe to drop." The teacher would walk the aisle, placing a paper face down on our desks. I would just stare at it, trying to recall anything that might be on the other side. I am, of course, talking about the always foreboding school exam. It was one of the worst feelings. My stomach was twisted in knots, the thoughts racing around in my head. Was I ready? Did I know my material? Did I study enough? No matter what the answers to those questions were, there were always doubts.

Today as I think back, I realize that those long-ago days in school taught me almost nothing that I needed to know as an adult to make it through life. Sure I learned English, without which would have made writing this book much harder. I learned as much math as I know, but I don't know as much math as they taught. I was instructed in science, for which I found some amount of fascination, but no desire to continue it as a career.

Because of Purpose

As I look back, they did not teach me about making it in life. I needed to know how to move from one rung of the career ladder to another. I desired to know about moving forward, how to succeed, or how to achieve the dreams I held for my life. Most importantly, they did not help me define what success was. As a favorite singing artist once said, "You can't teach what you don't know." No truer statement.

So, what was it all about? Why did I go to school? Was going to school a waste of time and effort?

No. Going to school was not a waste of time and effort. I am grateful to all of my teachers and for the education that I did manage to retain. We did learn things, useful things. One big key we all learned was that if we followed along with our material, determined to do the things appropriately enough, we could get a good grade. We also learned that life could be a series of steps, progressing upward, one thing compounding on another. Those steps took us from simple one plus one addition up to complex algebraic expressions and farther.

With this knowledge under our belt, we happily marched out into the world, and we were ready to take it on. Or so we thought. Unfortunately for most folks, yours truly included in that number, we were not as prepared as we thought we were. More importantly, we were not as ready as we needed to be but didn't know it.

In school, we learn the things that have been designed as a proper education by the average. The average see things as a middle ground. Not too high, but not too low. An "A" grade in school was not the top of life. It was the top of the average.

The most significant moment for me was when I learned that this is life, real day-to-day life. This is not a test. Everything we do matters, as well as everything we don't do. It all adds up,

Introduction

Throughout history, humankind has had dreams that drove them to achieve. These dreams supplied them with ambition and desire. The 'why' was always right there in front of them.

Things are different today for those who want to see their dreams become a reality. There is too much information and a ton of misinformation to weed through. The misinformation is the worst of it. Far too many people say they know how to make it happen, and typically they weave in the possibility that it can be an overnight success.

This book will never promise to make you an overnight success. There is discovery and effort involved. I will promise you that much. The main thing that this book can do is to show you how to achieve, cutting out all the fluff.

Within these pages, you will discover a way to find your purpose in life, how to kindle your dreams, fan the flames of desire, create a plan, and stay focused until you reach your goals.

Far too many years are wasted on faithless hoping and intangible wanting. I know because I was one of those people. At times I wanted a billion dollars, and other times I just wanted enough to live happy without having to go to a job each day. Both seemed out of reach.

In chapter one, you will read the story of how all of this came together. Chapters two and three lay an essential foundation that we will build on. Then, throughout the rest of this book, I will show you how to unlock your purpose and design a plan for your life so you too can create the future you want for you and your family.

This text will ask you to stretch and do new things. Commit right now to being open and ready for these tasks. You will need to search within yourself for where you want to be. Honesty will be required about where you are and what would really make you happy, not what the world says will make you happy.

It is my most sincere wish for you that you will achieve what you dream about. Take a slow deep breath and turn the page to a whole new life.

Vann

May the most you hope for be the least you get.

- Irish Proverb

---

and life hands us a grade, unfortunately for most, it is the grade we earned and not the grade we wanted.

I needed to stop wasting my time and figure this thing out. Why was I not climbing as well as I thought I should be? How can I do better? Where was the success I was told about?

Moreover, what was this thing called success? What was it, and why was it better than everything else? I didn't see anyone I knew have success.

We as human beings negotiate away half of our opportunities, half of our potential in life, at the front of all of our endeavors because we tend to aim at the middle. We aim for mediocrity, and we hit it.

- Mike Rayburn

Like the old Beatles song says, "Gonna try with a little help from my friends." Turning to my friends for an example did provide me with a great lesson, although not the one I was hoping for. As it turned out, my friends didn't have any more knowledge about what success was or how to get it. They went through the same schooling, read the same books, watched the same TV shows, and came out with mostly the same understanding of things as I did. I knew that I needed to understand more or something different, perhaps, and I wasn't gaining any knowledge from the people in the same boat as I was.

We were just floating along and hoping not to fall into the water. I needed to reach out and find something else.

The Beginning of the Beginning

Many years ago, I got excited about an opportunity that was to prove itself very beneficial in the long run. Still, it was not what it made itself out to be. Yet, I would not be where I am today without it. Another scrap in my life (You will learn about the "scraps" in our lives later in this chapter.)

A good beginning is half the work.

- Irish Proverb

A friend of mine introduced me to a 'business' design that I'm sure many of you have heard about. I'm not going to name it, but it has been around for several decades. The idea was that you sell a product. You build your business and get profit from it. Then you sell the business plan to others, which was one of the ways you grow your business. You help your folks do the same. Every time they sell something, you also get a piece of their action.

While it was an exciting idea, it fell flat in a few critical areas for me. They did one thing right, though. The people who were helping you get your business going would take you out to car dealerships and RV sales lots and help you 'dream build.' By that time in my life, I had totally lost or dropped all of the big ideas I had for the future.

There were conventions that you were to attend, small local ones, bigger regional ones, and large national ones. These were designed to pump you up and motivate the budding business owner as well as keep the old guard moving forward.

We worked the system, but we saw no one make a go of it. Even though we were getting help from those above us, we didn't see them making it either. Several levels up, there was no one making it, so what was the point. It reminded me of tossing spaghetti against a wall to see if it would stick. It was random, and there was no real path to follow. Yes, some did achieve various levels of success, but it was a very rare few. Besides, wealth wasn't the only thing I was after.

One of the things that they promoted was to read books on success. Ugh. I hated reading.

I remember the day, standing at the door. I was nervous. Honestly, I felt a little stupid and dorky, wondering what people would think when I went in and walked over 'there.' Could I? Should I?

The moment had come, and I could put it off no longer. Walking in, I was confronted with my greatest fear...being one of 'those' people. I walked back and found the aisle, just staring in disbelief at the vast number of titles before me.

You see, I was in the book store, standing in the area that I poked fun at the most, which was labeled the self-help aisle back then, but today are more aptly called personal transformation. This was the spot where the weird people went to find a book to tell them that they were alright and that everything was going to be just fine. Had I finally succumbed to that kind of need? Little did I understand that this was just the beginning for me, and, yes, it was what I needed to start this journey, but it was only a first step.

The vast array of titles amazed me. Some told me to think, some to believe, some to go for it, and others to just lay back and let it happen. This all seemed beyond my comprehension, but I wanted to find the answers. I just needed a little help, something that would point me in the right direction. As it turns out, that was my number one issue, but more on that later.

I did buy a few and began reading them, initially as part of the 'business' regime. Every book had different views regarding making it, the things that I needed to do, or things to think about. Some of these books were written by people years ago while others were written only a short time before. Some instructed me to focus on the problem, some wanted me to focus on a dream, and others lead me down a path of some daily or lifestyle customs to perform. Some said I wasn't organized enough, and while that was true, I wasn't sure how that could help me.

When the student is ready, the teacher shall appear.

- Unknown

In the end, I was no further along to finding what I needed, that being the answer to the ever-asking question. I felt lost and hopeless.

Because of Purpose

We stayed with the business for a few years, but after banging my head against that wall of the unknown, getting no real answers or direction, we bowed out. There were some good things I still remember from the tapes and conventions, but it felt like that was just a small piece of the picture I was trying to paint in my life.

There had to be more. I had a hole in my life, and it needed to be filled with something. It wasn't a marriage hole because we had been married for ten years at this point. It wasn't a family hole, not with two great children. It wasn't a career hole. I was tracking for a management line within the IT world.

It was so hard to put my finger on it. Something was missing, but I wasn't able to define it. I tried different things to fill that gap, but nothing was able to answer this question I had. It turned out that I wasn't able to define the problem very well, either. It felt hopeless.

The many self-help books that I read helped to give me a broad understanding of a few things, but again, no single book had the answer. They did give me a good overview of the human mind, the way we think, and how certain types of motivation works in our life.

I can't give you an exact number of the books I went through. Dare say it wasn't all of them or even a large percentage of them as their number is massive. I delved into books focused on business, leadership, winning, creating wealth, life organization, and positive mental attitude. Others concentrated on affirmations, creating valuable friendships, dreams and dreaming, and many biographies about people who've achieved.

Picking Up the Scraps in My Life

I kept asking myself why. Why am I still in this rut? What am I to do with all of my experiences and knowledge? A dear friend of mine, Darrin English of Plain English Ministries, says it best.

> *"When they all had enough to eat, He said to His disciples, "Gather the pieces that are leftover. Let nothing be wasted." (John 6:12 NIV)*
>
> *"Let nothing be wasted"...Scraps... that's what they collected that day—leftover pieces. The Bible doesn't say what they did with them. Maybe they fed the poor... perhaps they had a late-night snack... we're not sure. But what we do know is that they weren't wasted! There's a message in everything Jesus did, and the message here is CLEAR...God doesn't allow anything to go to waste in the life of one of His children...not even the scraps...the things in our lives we point to and say..." What was THAT all about?? THAT made NO sense! What a WASTE!" The unexpected financial burden...abuse suffered in the past...the untimely death of a loved one...SCRAPS!*
>
> *But what we didn't see was Jesus walking behind us all along, picking up every "scrap," collecting it for His purpose. Why? Because at some point in our life...sooner or later...Jesus reaches in His basket...pulls out one of our "scraps" and "feeds" someone who's hurting in your circle of influence! "If God can heal him...He can heal me! If God can provide for her...He can provide for me!" So...may God give us the grace to remember, the "scraps" of our lives are another*

person's "bread"! In the life of a believer, NOTHING is wasted!

That is my story in a Biblical nutshell. All of my history, my experiences, my knowledge, has led me to this place in my life. You see, it all came together on a trip one morning. *

A Moment of Clarity

It happened as my wife and I were on a short vacation in the Smoky Mountains. Holidays are times of resting the mind and sleeping in, except for me. My brain had an alarm clock built-in, and it went off every morning at 5:30 AM. And once it goes off, my mind starts up at full speed. There was no returning to sleep.

Having had this ailment, I called it, meant I had extra time alone before my wife woke up. With this spare time, I had decided to go into the living room of the cabin we rented and do some reading. I had been reading yet another book on this very subject and wanted to do some studying while I had the time.

Whether it was the quiet of the mountains, the time away from work, or my mind finally able to hear God screaming the answer to me, it started to happen. An incredible revelation began, and all of those pieces I had gathered through the years started to fall into place.

The quotes from people, the pages of the volumes I had read, the information stored away for later use all came to the surface. As the scraps were coming together, I could start to see the picture, the whole picture, for the very first time. The more I thought about it, the more the pieces fit together.

When my wife woke up, I shared with her what was going through my mind. The look on her face told me everything I needed to know. I was on to something. Each morning, additional pieces fit into place, and by the time that long weekend trip was up, it was taking shape.

We gotta be willing to adapt and change the way we believe about things, change our belief system to see what is capable for us moving forward.

- Lewis Howes

I began using this to change things in my life, climbing the corporate ladder and increasing my income more then I could have thought possible. Since then, I have been able to share this information with friends and family. Yes, it worked then and has continued to bring success and happiness into the lives of many. I knew that I needed to find a better avenue to share this incredible message and instruction, so *Because of Purpose* was born.

Ready?

Let me go ahead and tell you where some of you are.

Skepticism, in connection with ALL new ideas, is characteristic of all human beings.

- Napoleon Hill

You might be skeptical about what you are going to read. Can one book change your life? Would you be able to find something between these covers that will help you write a bigger and brighter future than the one you are facing right now?

I would encourage you to be open-minded and follow the instructions on these pages.

Remember, if you don't like where you are now, then you need to change what you are doing and how you are thinking.

You need to give yourself a chance. Just try it, no matter if you believe you can or not. You, as a person, are more than your thoughts. You are your actions. Let your actions tell you what you should believe about you. Follow through and begin to live the life you hunger for.

You are about to embark on a grand adventure that will affect the rest of your life. There are no more excuses. It is time for you to live your life and accomplish your dreams.

So, yes. Yes, you can. Let's get busy.

* This is a book about success and personal development. While you might have a different belief than I do regarding faith, I would encourage you not to pass up what you might be able to learn. Look for what you can glean from the text and allow it to teach. Leave behind what doesn't work for you.

Chapter 2

The Starting Point

From the Beginning

As with anything, the best place to start is right at the beginning. It might sound trivial, but it is definitely one of the greatest truths in life. Every path we take, every place we go, always begins somewhere, and also, it ends somewhere else. Within this book, I hope to be able to give you a new path to begin. Starting properly means getting to your destination. After all, why begin if you are not interested in finishing.

I remember recently passing a church that had on its marquee the following, "The wrong path will not get you to the right destination." Within the following pages, I will help you find not only the correct path but the correct destination. The one meant for you.

Before the Internet became what it is today, whenever we would go on a family trip, I would pull out a map and begin to plot our path. I would write down the waypoints, the miles, approximately how long it should take us to get to the next waypoint, and then I would measure that against the reality of our actual trip. The kids loved it because they found it entertaining, at least somewhat, and because they had something to look for, the next waypoint. It kept them mildly occupied.

I would never plot the route based on my favorite roads or using a direction I thought might be the most interesting. The course was always based on where we wanted to go because that's where the goal was.

IF YOU BEGIN HEADING IN A PARTICULAR DIRECTION AND FIND YOURSELF JUST A LITTLE BIT OFF, YOU WILL NEVER REACH YOUR GOAL.

Think of it this way. Let's say your destination is six hours away. If you are one degree off from traveling in the exact direction you need to, you will be six miles from your destination. So you can see that starting out right matters most. But the only way that you can start in the right direction and know that you will make it to your destination is to ensure that you know where you want to end up.

Besides knowing the right direction and understanding where you want to be in the end, we must define the starting point. The starting point is much more than just a place to begin. We need to understand precisely where we are at the beginning of any trip. If we don't, no matter what direction we believe is correct, we will not get to where we want to be.

There is an old saying that reads, "A journey of a thousand miles begins with a single step." While that is true, if we don't know where we are when we start the trip, we are likely headed in the absolute wrong direction. As vital as it is to have the endpoint defined, it is equally crucial to understand where we are before we begin the journey.

Yes, we are placing a lot of emphasis on the beginning of a journey. Understanding where we are starting from is essential to understanding how we can get to where we want to be.

If we look at a map believing that we are in Seattle and we want to travel to Miami, there are lots of ways to get there. The first thing we have to do is some evaluation to truly determine where we are at the beginning of a trip. Once our starting point has been established, then we work on our ending point.

Why?

One thing you are challenged with on this journey is establishing 'why.' If you are in Seattle and you want to get to Miami, it's always worth the time and the effort to ask yourself, why do you want to get to Miami? The reason for the journey is the 'purpose of the trip.'

Now that might sound a little bit odd. Typically the purpose of the journey, in our example, would be defined as getting to Miami. Just because our goal is getting to Miami doesn't mean that the purpose of the trip is reaching Miami. If we truly begin to examine the journey, there has to be a reason why. The purpose of the trip is wrapped up in the reason.

GOOD REASONS MAKE FOR GOOD ACTIONS BUT POWERFUL REASONS CREATE POWERFUL ACTIONS.

After all, there we are living in Seattle. We've been living in Seattle because of a reason. There was a reason that we were in Seattle, or still in Seattle if we grew up there, and there is a motive that has caused us to stay there. The reason for us staying there must now be overridden by a more significant or a higher purpose. Therefore our trip example must have a reason to get to Miami that is greater than the reason we are in Seattle. A trip like that can be expensive, take a lot of time, comes with risks, and will require lots of planning.

OUR DESIRE TO MOVE FORWARD MUST BE GREATER THAN OUR CONTENTMENT FOR STAYING PUT.

It is this reason, this desire, that has helped to create this book. Within the pages, you will hopefully find not only where you are, which you might already know, but where you genuinely want to be, and why you want to be there. Wherever it is you want to be, there must be a reason. Your reason doesn't have to be what others call success. It doesn't have to be based on fame, wealth, prestige, or anything else that someone might say is success. The term success might not be something that motivates you. Everyone's motivation is entirely different.

Many things might inspire an individual or a family to try such a feat. There are lots of people out there in the world that are driven by particular motivations that only they can speak to. I have no aspirations nor desire to climb Mount Everest, for example. I'm not saying that it is not a great thing to do. I'm saying it does not motivate me. What motivates one person to do one thing would usually not be the driving motivation for a different person to do their thing. Everybody's end result exists for varying reasons.

WHEN WE BEGIN TO UNDERSTAND THE REASONS, THE MOTIVATION AND THE PURPOSE, THEN WE CAN START TO UNDERSTAND WHY WE WANT TO GET TO OUR ENDPOINT.

It is a five-minute walk to my neighbor's house. Now, if you think about a typical suburb, five minutes sounds like a long time. I have to understand where their home is because I do not live in a typical suburban neighborhood. I cannot even see my neighbor's house at all from my house. I have to know where the endpoint is before I leave my house. If I don't, then the chances are that I will never make it, nor will I understand that I have made it if I do happen to arrive there. But why would I walk to my neighbor's house? That takes us back to purpose.

What is the End Point

As loosely defined by the dictionary, the endpoint is the completion of a process. Every journey must have an endpoint. Within the context of our discussion, the endpoint is where we want to end up. But that endpoint does not have to be limited to a single thing, a single place, or a single feeling.

Don't confuse the trip example we've used above to say that the endpoint is a particular thing. Fortunately, life is a lot more complex than that. It truly is much more complicated than that. One of the most incredible things about an endpoint is that not only do we get to define exactly what it is, what it looks like, and what it feels like, but we can change it as many times as we want. We can also have multiple endpoints for the different facets of our life.

Many times when we hear motivational speakers impress upon us about a dream we have in life, it is typically wrapped up in material things like a car, a boat, or a house. There is absolutely nothing wrong with any of these things being an endpoint. As you move through this material, hopefully, you'll see that an endpoint can be significantly grander than just the simple material things that we look at here in life.

Many times we think of an endpoint or goal, as a material thing. That is perfectly fine. Most people start out that same way. Why? Simple. Actually, that is the answer. Because it is simple.

Let's say you are going down the street and you see a car in the style and color that you like, and you feel something. So many of my friends can tell you what their exact dream car would be. They can describe it down to the accessories that it would have, the details of lights, the types of rims, the type of stereo system, or even how the steering wheel would feel in their hand.

Sometimes it is easier to grasp on to the goals of the tangible things when the journey is new to us. We understand that a journey like this is more than just the keys of a car, house, or boat. Yet it is something that we can all understand, and the endpoint is easy to define.

We need to know where we are when we begin our journey, and we need to be able to define the endpoint easily.

I am not asking you to figure out where you are in life, nor am I asking you to define where you want to be or picture the goals or dreams you may have in life. This chapter is about building the groundwork so that we understand four essential concepts. We need to realize that

1. We have a place to begin
2. There will be a place we want to go
3. There will be a reason to get there
4. There will be specific actions required to achieve it

Why the Dream

It even bothers me to use the term dream. Many times, a dream is just that, a dream, something never achieved.

In this book, when we think about a dream, we are talking about something beautiful. It might be a new car, or perhaps a vintage car. Maybe it's a once-in-a-lifetime vacation, probably to somewhere exotic or somewhere unique. Perhaps for you, it is a particular lifestyle. Not necessarily a lifestyle of opulence and luxury, maybe it's one surrounded by the love of family, or safety, or peace.

As in our traveling example, there had to be a reason we wanted to get to Miami. Miami would be the dream or endpoint. The reason would be needed to create action. The stronger the reason, or purpose in our case, the stronger the motivation would be to complete the tasks before us.

The dream is essential. Do not lose sight of this simple truth. If you do not have a goal right now, all the more reason you need to continue reading this book. It's time to wake up your dreams.

Your time is limited, so don't waste it living someone else's life.

- Steve Jobs

Because of Purpose

Chapter 3

How the Mind Works

In this chapter, we are going to look at how this marvelous mind we have functions. There are a lot of mysteries as to how our brain is wired, and when we understand more about how our mind functions, we can do more with it.

The first and foremost thing to understand about our brain is that it is NOT working against us. It has a set of policies that govern it. A policy is a set of principles used to guide decisions or processes. No matter what you are doing or how your life is right now, it is so because of the way your brain functions.

Someone once explained it like this. No matter what is going on in life, you are winning. I know you might disagree at first, I sure did, but allow me to explain. The mind is only wired to win. The issue is what you are winning at is based on your own rules and life experiences. I'll explain the file cabinet and history in just a moment.

As an example, let's look at a common issue, that of weight loss. If you believe deep down that diets don't work, or you can only last a few days with a new food plan, and your history proves it, then your brain is going to respond to that. It will see situations or create issues that are consistent with what you believe and know from your past. When your brain does this, it thinks you are winning. You are achieving what you believe to be true for you.

Our only limitations are those we set up in our own minds.

- Napoleon Hill

It becomes quickly evident that we need to find a way to turn this around. When we get our thinking heading the right direction, it gives us the power to get through anything in life.

The Mind Circles

I want you to think of the inner workings of your mind as if there were two levels to it. At the top level, we have the thinking or rational level. The thinking level is where we make a decision. At the second level is the automatic level. The automatic level heavily influences the decisions that we make at the top level.

The automatic level is very efficient at what it does. Too good in some cases. But, with a bit of know-how and some time, you can make it work to help you succeed in life.

I see the automatic level of our brains as a set of three circles. Each of these circles has a name and a function. The circle at the top of the hierarchy is called the calculator. One of the other two is called the file cabinet, and the last one is our history.

Now, place these three circles in a triangle with each circle at one of the three corners. The calculator at the top corner, and the other two are at the bottom corners. Let's start by digging into the file cabinet.

File Cabinet

You probably already know what a file cabinet is. It is a large box or rectangle, typically made out of metal or wood, that holds important papers. These papers are organized into subjects or topics. The file cabinet is one large repository broken down to drawers and further into separate areas with folders in each of the drawers.

If you keep your bills organized in your file cabinet, you might have folders for the utility bills, car note, mortgage, or insurance. You might also keep instructions books for stuff you've bought, warranty information, tax documents, and who knows what. After you have all of that stuff in there, it stays in there until you need it.

In our home, we go through the file cabinet once a year and pull out the old stuff. This creates space for the coming year's information, allows us to weed out the things no longer needed, and to put things away into storage for tax purposes.

Back to the mind circles, we have a file cabinet. This file cabinet is there to store some significant pieces of information. The information inside the file cabinet of our brain is what I will call the rules. What rules? Our rules. The ones that are just for us. These are the rules we live our life by.

These rules are the things that we believe about ourselves. Everything that we think we can do and everything that we trust we cannot do is stored in the file cabinet. This is a collection of things we've been told through our childhood, teenage years, and as an adult. This collection includes both the good and the bad.

Just like an actual file cabinet, the file cabinet of our mind does not evaluate anything. There is no validation process. Good or bad, right or wrong, things are filed away until called for later.

We can open an ordinary filing cabinet and pull out whatever we no longer want or need in there. The file cabinet of our mind works differently. The only way to get the bad stuff out is to put good things in it. We will talk about that in chapter eight, Daily Habits.

Our History

The next circle at the bottom of the triangle is also a place where things are stored away. This one is called Our History. The historic area of our brain tucks away all of our life experiences. All of our successes and failures, good times and bad, that we have had in our life reside here. It doesn't matter if it's big things or small things, it will find a home here.

Like the file cabinet, the history circle does not judge anything or try to put it in perspective. Our history has already been written. The thoughts and the emotions associated with those events are set in stone. The amount of emotion related to an event gives it a factor that can cause it to be something from meanless to massively impactful. The stronger the feelings associated with the event, the more impactful it becomes.

The Calculator

The last circle, the one at the top of the triangle, I call The Calculator. This is not a place that does any judging or weighing in on things. Remember, these three areas all reside in the automatic level or our minds. Now, within the calculator, you will find simple, straightforward math. Addition is the simplest form of math, which is a perfect way to describe this part of our brain.

The calculator does two things. One is to request information from the file cabinet and our history, and the other is to add those two things together. Simple, yes?

It Works Like This

Here is how this works. You are confronted with a situation. Your thinking or rational level of your brain asks the calculator to give some feedback on the issue at hand. The calculator happily springs into action and requests information related to the situation from our file cabinet and our history. The results come back, are added together in the calculator, and past to the thinking part of our brain.

Let's use an example from my life. Plumbing.

Growing up, I was never exposed to any plumbing jobs. The amount of information I had regarding the subject was absolutely nothing. I wasn't afraid of trying it. I just knew zero about how to design or install plumbing. In this case, it was a garbage disposal for our first home.

I got the disposal, the needed plumbing pieces according to the instructions, and proceeded to crawl under the sink. For whatever reason, things didn't line up quite right. I did the best I could. You have to remember this was 1987, and YouTube wasn't even a glimmer in its creator's eye. After finding that the plumbing leaked, I got the only things I had on hand: room temperature vulcanizing putty and F4 tape. These are used to seal aircraft hydraulic hoses. I figured it should work for this simple application.

I slowed the leak enough to call it good and resigned myself to keep a small trash can under there, dumping it out weekly. It was hardly an ounce of water each week, so I was OK with it, and my new bride was happy to have a garbage disposal. Win-win. I figured that I could ask some folks about it later and deal with it then.

We Become What We Think About. Our entire lives are guided by our minds. The thoughts we allow into our brains every day shape our lives, and determine our future.

- Earl Nightingale

Everything was great until my dad and grandpa came out for a visit. I asked them where things might have gotten off track during my installation, opening up the doors under the sink. (*insert sound of small explosion here*)

Obviously, what I did was wrong. Honestly, I knew that already. I just needed a little help in understanding what and why. Then I was going to fix it. My dad and grandpa took it upon themselves to first verbally tear apart my handy work, then tear apart the installation of the disposal. They reinstalled it and had it leak-free after several hours of labor under the sink. I can neither confirm nor deny that a few choice words might have been said while trying to scrape off the F4 tape and RTV.

This did two things. One it filled my file cabinet with "I can't do plumbing" and attached strong negative feelings to an event for my history circle.

Since that day, plumbing was my nemesis. Every plumbing job I attempted went horribly wrong. Things didn't fit, over tightened and broke pieces, didn't get the right parts, it always leaked no matter what, you name it. Anything and everything plumbing related went sideways on me. Until...

One day, in a different house, many years later, my wife begged me to have the plumbing fixtures for the washing machine moved from under the stairs and installed into the back room. I couldn't blame her, though. Getting in and out of the under stairs closet with a basket of clothes was ridiculous. I agreed to crawl under the house and take a look. It was copper pipes. Thinking to myself, copper plumbing is not like regular plumbing; it's soldering. I can solder electronics perfectly. I should be able to do this.

I crawled into our eighteen-inch crawlspace and soldered everything up, no leaks, first time. I loved working with, and still do, copper plumbing. The difference was having something else that I could relate too.

I have been holding a soldering iron since I was eight. I understood how solder works and the importance of flux. A few weeks prior, I already had a positive experience with sweating copper joints from building a ham radio antenna.

To this day, if a project comes up and plumbing is involved, I always ask, "Is it copper, or is it plumbing?"

Recently, because of a decided heart, I tackled a project that I was not sure about. I had to replace the subfloor under the toilet in one of our bathrooms. Demolition was no problem. Rebuilding the floor wasn't either. I got the new linoleum glued down without significant issues. Now the toilet.

I paused and thought about the times it went badly, and a few minor wins along the way. I was going to get into this slowly, one step at a time, not get frustrated. I was going to beat this. I was reprogramming my file cabinet. I got the wax ring down, the toilet in place and level. The water connection was made, and...no leaks. I had done it. Now I also had a positive experience to put in my history. It worked and didn't drip anywhere that it wasn't supposed to.

After that successful event, I realized that we link comfort and discomfort to the wrong things. Comfort would have been having someone else do the repair. Instead, I began to create a link between plumbing and comfort.

Comfort vs. Uncomfort

If you have spent any time on the Internet, you know what a hyperlink is. It is some text or a graphic that has code behind it. When you click on the hyperlink, you are directed to a different page.

As humans, we tend to link things to comfort or discomfort based on our experiences or ideas in our file cabinet. I know people who were told as children that dogs are vicious. We had a lady in our house once, and our cat jumped into her lap, looking for a new friend. She flipped out. Her mother told her that cats always go for the eyes.

I had a strong discomfort association with auto maintenance. No real reason, but it was there. I had to change that by creating new entries for auto maintenance in my file cabinet and then getting some positive experiences in my history.

We can also see other types of links we tend to have in life. One very familiar one is food. We associate, or link, certain foods or food types with comfort or discomfort. There is even a food category called comfort foods. These are supposed to make you feel better, and a lot of people turn to them in times of stress, facing a problem, or even bored.

A Negative mind will never give you a positive life.

- Lewis Howes

During the pandemic, which is still going strong at the time I wrote this, there was an increase in people's weight during the lockdowns. People were concerned about catching the virus, or they were under state orders, so they were home with little to do but watch TV and snack. I turned in a different direction. Watching what I ate and working out more, I lost weight. That became my comfort because I made that association differently than others did.

Addictions to various things are also part of this comfort link. Drugs and alcohol can become associated with comfort, although they tend to leave things in a bigger mess.

Chapter eight is going to get into how to change what is in your file cabinet. But for now, just understand the math. For me, plumbing was a negative experience and had malicious entries in my file cabinet. When the calculator gets its hands on those two negative thoughts, it is added together and comes out negative. Our rational brain uses that, and then, because the mind is wired to win, amplifies the feelings and saves us from doing any plumbing. If you do attempt it, it goes horribly wrong, and we say something like, "See? I told you I couldn't do plumbing." Your mind thinks you won!

If you can build up some positive in your file cabinet about something, you will begin to offset the experiences in your history.

WITH A DEFINITE PURPOSE TO CHANGE YOUR MIND AND OFFSET YOUR PAST, YOU CAN CHANGE YOUR FUTURE FOREVER AND FOR THE BETTER.

The good thing is that you CAN decide to change your future for the better. Just reading this book is proof of that.

Chapter 4

Finding what Matters

In Chapter Two, we discussed this journey of achieving your goals, comparing it to a trip. We needed to know where we were starting from and where we wanted to go. This chapter is dedicated to understanding your starting point.

Some may say that it doesn't matter where you begin. Only the place you end up is what matters most. The issue is that you MUST understand where you are right now so you can know better how to get to where you want to be.

Finding Your Positive Triggers

In the last chapter, we discussed how your brain is wired to win. It is essential to understand this part of the picture. Now, we are going to look at how YOU are wired. Knowing this will begin to show you several important things about you, your goals, and why you make some of the decisions you do.

Some things excite you, and some things you tend to shy away from. This is normal for everyone. As an example, if you are doing something special tomorrow, whatever it might be, and you are all for it, you are excited. You might even have trouble sleeping the night before.

Another thing that might keep you up at night is something you really don't want to do or go through. The next day is destined to be terrible or uncomfortable. You again lose sleep, but you also have a knot in your stomach. This future event or set of circumstances you find yourself in is called a trigger.

A trigger is an incident or situation that can cause you to be very distressed or even lead to negative self-talk, anxiety, panic, or even depression. We are going to call these negative triggers.

On the other hand, the things that excite you we call a positive trigger. This is something that 'triggers' you emotionally but pleasantly. A positive trigger can cause you to smile, enjoy things even more, have fun, and laugh. The good news is, we are going to talk about your positive triggers in this chapter.

I enjoy sci-fi. Growing up, Star Trek (The Original Series) was on the TV. I also grew up at the beginning of the Star Wars series. One thing that confused me, though, was how characters could walk up to the controls of a ship they had never seen before, with writing on it they didn't know, and tell it was the navigation system. If you don't know the language, then you don't know what you are looking at.

Finding your positive triggers is critical to helping you move forward on your journey. If your goals and your positive triggers align, they are speaking the same language. Also, understanding how your personality is wired makes it easier to define your goals, and it will also serve as a safety check. We will talk more about that in a bit.

Because of Purpose

These triggers are what I call your life attributes. In this context, an attribute is a trait of someone. It is something that they do or can be used to describe what they are like. When we talk about your life attributes, we are going to look for the things that make you want to get up in the morning, those things that agree with you the most.

What is the opposite of happiness? Sadness? No. Just as love and hate are two sides of the same coin, so are happiness and sadness. Crying out of happiness is a perfect illustration of this. The opposite of love is indifference, and the opposite of happiness is - here's the clincher - boredom.

- Timothy Ferris

In the following pages, you will find a list of over four hundred life attributes. Your job is to read through every one. When you find something that catches your fancy, write it down. I would suggest that you not mark in this book as you will come back to this list several times through the coming years. Your life attributes will shift over time as you change and as your situation changes.

It's always good to review your life attributes every two or three years, at least. When you have a big event happen like reaching an important goal, moving into your new home, or any significant shift in your life, you will want to give it a few weeks and then review your life attribute list. Each time you go over the list, follow precisely the same instructions.

The focus is to narrow down this list from over four hundred attributes to forty to fifty. Do not let your list exceed fifty items, but make sure you have at least thirty. Go ahead and do this now.

Abundance	Agility	Attractiveness
Acceptance	Alertness	Authority
Accessibility	Altruism	Autonomy
Accomplishment	Ambition	Availability
Accountability	Amusement	Awareness
Accuracy	Animals	Balance
Achievement	Anti-bureaucratic	Beauty
Activity		Being the best
Adaptability	Appreciation	Belonging
Advancement	Approachability	Benevolence
Adventure	Assertiveness	Boldness
Advocacy	Attention to detail	Bravery
Affection		Brotherhood
Affluence	Attentiveness	Brilliance

Because of Purpose

Calmness	Competitive	Creativity
Candor	Completion	Credibility
Capable	Composure	Cunning
Caring	Comprehensive	Curiosity
Caution	Concentration	Customer focus
Certainty	Confidence	Daring
Challenge	Confidential	Decency
Change	Conformity	Decisive
Charity	Connection	Dedication
Cheerfulness	Consciousness	Delight
Citizenship	Consistency	Democratic
Cleanliness	Contentment	Dependability
Clear	Continuity	Depth
Cleverness	Contribution	Determination
Collaboration	Control	Development
Comfort	Conviction	Devotion
Commitment	Cooperation	Different
Common Sense	Coordination	Dignity
Communication	Cordiality	Diligence
Community	Correct	Directness
Compassion	Courage	Discipline
Compatibility	Courtesy	Discovery
Competence	Craftsmanship	Discretion
Competition	Creation	Diversity

Because of Purpose

Dominance	Equality	Fitness
Down-to-earth	Ethical	Flair
Dreaming	Excellence	Flexibility
Drive	Excitement	Focus
Duty	Exhilarating	Foresight
Eagerness	Exotic	Forgiveness
Economy	Experience	Formal
Ecstasy	Expertise	Fortitude
Education	Exploration	Freedom
Effectiveness	Expressiveness	Friendship
Efficiency	Extravagance	Frugality
Elegance	Exuberance	Fulfillment
Empathy	Fairness	Fun
Empower	Faith	Generosity
Encouragement	Faithfulness	Giving
Endurance	Family	Global
Energy	Famous	Goodness
Engagement	Fashion	Goodwill
Enjoyment	Fast	Grace
Entertainment	Fearless	Gratitude
Enthusiasm	Feelings	Greatness
Entrepreneurship	Ferocious	Growth
	Fidelity	Guidance
Environment	Firm	Happiness

Because of Purpose

Hard work	Inquisitive	Local
Harmony	Insight	Logic
Health	Inspiration	Longevity
Helpful	Integrity	Love
Heroism	Intelligence	Loyalty
History	Intensity	Mastery
Holiness	International	Maturity
Honesty	Intimacy	Meaning
Honor	Intuition	Meekness
Hope	Invention	Mellow
Hospitality	Investing	Merit
Humility	Inviting	Meticulous
Humor	Joy	Mildness
Imagination	Justice	Mindfulness
Impact	Kindness	Moderation
Impartial	Knowledge	Modesty
Improvement	Lawful	Money
Inclusiveness	Leadership	Motivation
Independence	Learning	Mystery
Individuality	Legal	Neatness
Industry	Leisure	Nerve
Influence	Liberty	Obedience
Informal	Listening	Open-minded
Innovation	Lively	Optimism

Because of Purpose

Order	Positive	Quality
Organization	Potency	Quietness
Originality	Potential	Rational
Participation	Power	Realistic
Partnership	Practical	Reason
Passion	Pragmatic	Recognition
Patience	Precise	Recreation
Patriotism	Precision	Refined
Peace	Preparedness	Reflection
People	Present	Relationships
Perception	Preservation	Relaxation
Perfection	Pride	Reliability
Performance	Privacy	Resilience
Perseverance	Proactive	Resolute
Persistence	Productivity	Resourcefulness
Personal development	Professionalism	Respect
	Profits	Responsibility
Persuasive	Progress	Responsiveness
Philanthropy	Prosperity	Rest
Playfulness	Prudence	Restraint
Pleasantness	Punctuality	Results
Poise	Purity	Reverence
Polish	Purpose	Rigor
Popularity	Pursuit	Risk

Because of Purpose

Sacrifice	Simplicity	Temperance
Safety	Sincerity	Tenderness
Sanitary	Skillfulness	Thankfulness
Satisfaction	Smart	Thorough
Security	Solitude	Thoughtful
Self-awareness	Spirit	Timeliness
Self-motivation	Spirituality	Tolerance
Self-responsibility	Spontaneous	Touch
Self-control	Stability	Tough
Self-directed	Standardization	Toughness
Self-reliance	Status	Traditional
Selflessness	Stealth	Training
Sense of humor	Stewardship	Tranquility
Sensitivity	Strength	Transparency
Sensuality	Structure	Travel
Serenity	Success	Trust
Serious	Support	Truth
Service	Surprise	Understanding
Sharing	Sustainability	Unflappable
Shrewd	Sympathy	Uniqueness
Significance	Synergy	Unity
Silence	Talent	Universal
Silliness	Teamwork	Useful
	Teaching	Utility

Because of Purpose

Valor

Value

Variety

Victory

Vigor

Virtue

Vision

Vitality

Warmth

Watchfulness

Wealth

Welcoming

Well-Being

Willfulness

Winning

Wisdom

Wonder

Work/life balance

Count them up. You want between thirty and fifty attributes selected before you continue past this point. If you have them, congratulations. This is a significant step toward understanding how you will be successful.

You need to pick your attributes before I reveal a little secret I am about to tell you. At the beginning of this book, I made a promise. I was going to help you find your purpose in life. Your life attributes are going to help define this.

One of my life attributes is teaching. I love it. It excites me to share some knowledge that I have with others. This book is a passion of mine because of this. Being able to help someone create the life that they want pushes me on to spend long hours in my home office and type each word and each sentence. It is part of my purpose in life to share and teach.

Even more people today have the means to live, but no meaning to live for.

- Viktor Frankl

Narrowing Your Focus

Now that you have your list of thirty to fifty attributes, we are going to work on a little exercise to help you narrow them down. We have taken the list from over four hundred and narrowed that down to between thirty to fifty attributes. Now we will thin that list down some more.

Because of Purpose

Whatever number of attributes that you ended up with, we are going to drop it even more. If you have thirty to forty attributes, you will narrow the list down to twenty. If you have forty to fifty, you will narrow the list down to twenty-five.

Here is how you will narrow it down. As you scan through the list, you may find a word that means more to you than other words on the list. Mark that one so you know that it is one you want to keep, but don't cross out any of the other words. You will need them in a moment.

When you have completed that, you should have a list with your twenty to twenty-five most meaningful life attributes marked. Go back to the words you have not marked and look for words that mean the same as those you have marked. Write these related words behind the words that you marked. I have an example for you here.

Let's say that a portion of my list included hope, joy, knowledge, leisure, peace, relaxation, and teaching. As I look at the words, some might mean about the same thing. Remember, the terms only need to mean the same thing to me, not to a dictionary, a thesaurus, or anyone else.

I would mark joy and teaching as they mean more to me than the other related words on the list. I would write hope after joy and knowledge after teaching. As I continued to work on the list, I would also write leisure after peace, because peace means more to me than leisure.

I started with a list of seven words and end up with this list:

Joy – Hope

Peace – Leisure, Relaxation

Teaching – Knowledge

Because of Purpose

What we have done is not only narrowed the list down but also started to build definitions for the words that represent our life attributes the best. Your challenge is to do the same. Take your time. It's alright if you need a few hours to do this. You want to make sure it is right for you. Remember your target numbers and begin.

Are you done?

One more time, you are to narrow the list down. I can hear you moaning and groaning from here, but trust me. When we are done, you will understand why we needed to do it this way.

You are going to take the list down to the most meaningful ten words. As you see additional words that can be grouped together, do that just as you did in the previous exercise.

Keep the most important and meaningful words in the front and write the rest behind it. It's OK if you have a word without similar words, but ask yourself if you might revisit that word. If it meant so much, why is it all alone? If you leave it, that's fine. If you change it, that's fine. If you go back to the master list and pull out one or two, that's also fine. If the result matches as described below, you are on track.

Yes, this will be the last narrowing of the list.

Again, take your time. There is no pass or fail as long as you end up with a list that makes you smile. Go for it.

Are you finished?

Read through your list. Read aloud the ten words from your list. Does it make you feel something? Are you smiling? If not, review it again. If it does, CONGRATULATIONS.

Because of Purpose

You may count yourself among the few who know this much about themselves. I am very proud of you for completing this exercise. It can be taxing, but you did it!

You now have a list of ten words, some or all with definitions that you built, that describe your positive triggers, your life attributes. These words represent how you are wired, and they show you what your purpose is in life.

For me, teaching was one of my attributes and my most meaningful. I get a charge out of it. For years, I have always shared the things that I've learned and done. I have helped people design and install solar power systems in their homes, build aquaponic systems, do carpentry, and a host of other things. I love to teach. When I have a speaking engagement the next day, I am so excited about it that I lose some sleep.

Teaching is one of the things that drives me. Another one is adventure. Next to adventure are the words excitement, travel, and recreation. I have a big goal to sail around to every island nation in the Caribbean. It matches adventure, travel, and excitement.

Your list is for you. It is likely only to match you. These are your life attributes, and it helps you to define your purpose in your life. Now, let's see what we can do with them.

Chapter 5

Your Dreams

Understanding Your Dreams

Dreams are an essential ingredient in the recipe for success. Your dreams are the target you aim at, and they are the desire of your heart. Without having dreams to aspire for, you wouldn't have anything to be excited about or to strive towards.

While dreams are marvelous, they are a double-edged sword. A dream can inspire you to action, or it can cause you to get lost along the way. If your dream is worth going for, you will run hard after it and enjoy having achieved it. If your dream is lofty and not well defined, you will jog around for a bit, slow down to a walk, and finally stop, never getting near your destination.

Four things are needed for a dream to be a goal. You must have a well-defined dream, you must do a life attribute check to make sure it is a goal for you, versus doing it for someone else, you will need a plan, and you must have dates. Let's look at the first one, a very clear dream.

If you ask someone what they want for their future, they may tell you that they want to be rich, or they want a big house, or fast cars, or whatever their fancy might be. While those things are enjoyable, it isn't a good picture of the future. When people say those things, it paints a nebulous picture, or better yet, they are painting on a cloud.

An artist will tell you that paint doesn't stick to a cloud. Why? It has no real substance. For those who are trying to build their future with a statement like I want to be rich, their hopes and dreams won't stick either.

Take a group of people who all say that they want a fast car. Ask them which one, and most of them will probably know which one they want. Maybe a hypercar, like a Bugatti Chiron, blue and black carbon fiber, with chrome accents. Wait, what? I got lost for a moment. A few won't know precisely what they want, so they have to leave the group.

Ask them which options they want in it, and the crowd narrows a bit more. They don't know. Ask them if they know the exact MSRP of the car equipped the way they want it, and the number of folks you are talking to drops even more. Then ask them if they have a picture of it hanging on a vision board in their home with a date they want it by, and at this point, you might be standing alone.

It's the same thing with other dreams. What does rich mean? How much money equals a rich? One million, two million, ten million? Now is that money in a bank somewhere, or is that income per year? What is a big house? How many square feet, or bedrooms, or floors?

I met a man who said he wanted to be rich. I asked him how rich did he want to be. He said, "Very rich." I asked him how he was going to make that money. "I don't know.", he said. There isn't enough paint in that statement to color a future with.

You need to have a vivid description of your dream. Remember, this will not be a fantasy. It will be something you will turn into your reality. You should be able to describe it in detail. Write it down. This is the beginning of turning your dreams into your future.

Don't let the size of your dream scare you. If this is the first time you have gone after a dream, most things will appear a little looming. You might have heard a great acrostic for the word fear. False Evidence Appearing Real. That fear you might experience is just that. False. It is scary because you have never done anything like this before.

Your dream is on the other side of your fear.

- Vann Lantz

Get your dreams down on paper. Get online and print out some pictures that look like your dream. Cut up some magazines for things that go with the description of your dream. Hold on to those photos because you will need them in a few chapters.

As an example, here is a dream in full detail.

> *My dream is a small beachfront house. It is raised on tall pilings with a full wrap-around porch. The part of the porch that faces the sea is bigger than the rest. There is a small jacuzzi for five under the patio roof on the sea-facing porch. The house is two stories tall, with two guest*

Because of Purpose

bedrooms and a full bathroom downstairs, a big kitchen, and a great room. There is no carpet because of the sand but some excellent tile flooring throughout. The master bedroom is the only thing upstairs, with its private bathroom and walk-in closet. There is a small patio upstairs, just out the sliding glass door. From the main deck, there is a set of stairs that go up above the master bedroom to the crow's nest for the most incredible views and gorgeous sunsets.

WOW! I think I might be ready to move into that dream right now! Sounds fantastic, doesn't it? How good would it sound if it read A two-story beach house with a big porch and a view? Pretty vague and weak, right?

Having an unusually large goal is an adrenaline infusion that provides the endurance to overcome the inevitable trials and tribulations that go along with any goal.

- Timothy Ferris

YOUR DREAMS DESERVE GREAT DETAIL,
AND DON'T FORGET THE PICTURES!

Matching Dreams to Attributes

Writing down your dreams might have been a little scary. It makes it real, doesn't it? Also, wanting that house or trip, or whatever your fancy, it can seem monumental. Some of my dreams are mammoth and do give me a certain amount of pause when I see them written down. But I am headed toward them at full speed. I am fully committed.

From the previous chapter, you have figured out what your life attributes are, and now you have some dreams written down. Basically, when you look at our trip example from chapter two, you have figured out where you are starting from, and you have an understanding of where you want to go. Congratulations. With just those two things, you have accomplished more than most folks on earth have when considering or planning for their future. But this is just the start.

Knowing where you are starting and where you might want to go is not a place to stop. More is needed.

Look at your dreams list. When you do, I know you have several emotions that go through your mind. Some of them might be stronger than others, both good and bad. When the feelings are good and robust, it is likely a dream that you can get behind one hundred percent. This dream motivates you and can even provoke you to action.

On the other side of that same situation is where the problems can exist. Having your life attributes, you can weed out the dreams that aren't 'you.' What I mean by that is sometimes we can inherit or adopt the dreams of others. These are not your dreams, but those that you might have brought on board, now on your list, which can cause you to stumble because they aren't your dreams.

Because of Purpose

If the dream isn't yours, and you are early in your success journey, it will lack the same luster for you, and you might not have the same drive to achieve it. You need for your beginning goals to be ones that not only make you stretch, but they are those that are yours. You need to nurture the zeal that you feel behind your goals. Without that passion, you can lose motivation, slow down, and even stop chasing that goal.

With your newly comprised list of dreams and your life attributes with their definitions, you can do a sanity or safety check. When you think about one of the dreams on your list, visualize what it would be like to achieve that goal. How many of your life attributes match the feelings that you have when you visualize having achieved the goal?

Perhaps it was your parents who said they want a cabin in the woods or your spouse who wishes that they had the chance to explore Europe for two weeks. Whatever it might be, even with the best intentions, at the beginning of your success journey, and this might sound bad, you need to be a little selfish.

Before you slam the book closed and toss it across the room, give me a moment to explain.

As I said, you need all of your emotions behind the goal to be solid and full. They are going to help you to move along. If the dream is someone else's, it might not do that for you. If it does, and you think it will last until the very end, then, by all means, go for it. Most of the time, it is not true, but you know you best. Do what you know to be the perfect fit for you.

Look at your first goal. I can clearly remember mine. It was to pay off the credit card way ahead of schedule if I just paid the minimums. I would sell things, put all or most of the tax refund against it, and do some odd jobs and crafts to sell. It was the joy and feeling of financial freedom that was driving me each day.

What attributes are on your list that will keep you on track and on time? Is it just one of the ten, or several? Write those next to your dream. When you need a little boost, read your dream out loud, look at the pictures, and imagine it happening right now. Then recite each attribute out loud in a positive statement.

"It is the feeling of joy and financial freedom pushing me each day until this credit card is paid off early."

Now, go through each of your dreams and match up your life attributes. If you have a dream that doesn't match any life attributes, you might consider setting that one aside and think about why it is a dream on your list.

If you are comfortable where you are, then you're not fighting hard enough, you're not pushing yourself enough. So being uncomfortable is a good thing.

- Dan – from the YouTube channel Sailing Uma

Final Thoughts on Dreams

Until now, your dreams have just been fairy tales. Thoughts and stories that would never come to be. They were the soft and fuzzy clouds in the sky that you can't paint on.

As of this moment, your dreams have a place, a real place, in your life.

You have written them down on paper. They have moved from the imaginary place in your mind to being actual words on a real piece of paper.

Your dreams have a purpose. If they didn't, why would you hold on to them or keep thinking about them? They are there to tell you that you can, and a better life awaits you. They are also there to push you.

When I was first learning to drive, my dad had an old beat-up Datsun 620 pick up truck. It was a mess. One bench seat, tight cab, and I painted it with spray paint. I can't believe I drove that truck with a smile on my face.

There were a few things wrong with it. The battery would not start it every few starts, so it had to be push started. A few of my friends would get it rolling, and I would dump the clutch, hoping that the transmission or engine wouldn't dump at the same time.

It was the push that the truck needed to get the engine turned over enough to fire it up. When you need a little push to get your engine started up again, just read over your dreams and look at your goals. That is what they are for. Tomorrow the sun will rise and await to see what you will accomplish.

DREAMS ARE BEAUTIFUL THINGS, BUT EVEN MORE SO WHEN YOU BEGIN TO REALIZE THAT YOURS ARE NOT JUST PRETTY THOUGHTS, THEY ARE BECOMING YOUR REALITY.

If your dreams seem large and unclimbable, just remember what they are there for. They are the arrival signs for the places you are going to. Dreams give us the push and motivation we need in the moments we lose our traction.

They can seem scary. When you are first trying to gain your footing on your path, everything is new and different. You can be uncomfortable at times. It is only because you are doing that which you have never attempted. Push through to your first finish line, and you will find the inspiration to tackle the next one.

Trust me. It isn't as scary a place as it seems.

I would like for people to stop being so scared... Whenever I talk to someone about sailing, they always say to me, "Aren't you afraid of pirates?" And if it's not pirates, its sharks. "What about the sharks? Aren't you afraid of the sharks?"
I would like, if anything, during my career online to displace that illogical attitude which constricts possibilities and imagination. If you are to go sailing or follow your dreams, or do whatever it is that you want to do, there is a 100% chance of having some time onboard or whatever it is that you are doing, that is so good that it will change your life and that you will talk about forever. There are also many difficult times but generally speaking, no pirates.

If you have 10 or 50 or 1000 attempts at different things over the course of your life, eventually one of them will pay off. This could be sailing or traveling or starting a company or approaching that guy or girl that you have been keen on for months. It doesn't really matter. What I'm saying here is that the world is a much less scary place than it is made out to be.

- Riley Whitelum – From the YouTube channel Sailing la Vagabonde

---

Because of Purpose

Chapter 6

Mapping it Out

Before you starting drawing the pathway to your dreams, let's talk about what your dreams ask of you.

The first thing they ask is that you believe that you can achieve. You need to believe in yourself. You CAN get everything that you set your mind to accomplish. This will be discussed in greater detail in a later chapter. Understand at this point that belief in yourself is essential, and I will show you how to gain what you need.

The second thing that your dreams ask of you is action. Without action, you can't make any ground toward your dreams. If you sat in a car in Seattle and did nothing, no matter how good your written path to Miami is, you will never get there.

There is no such thing as something for nothing. For you to gain or achieve your goals, you must be willing to give something in return, and you get to go first. You give, and the world responds by giving you your dreams. You are and have something of value. Your time and gifts are that very thing. Use them and make a difference.

Also keep in mind as you begin to build your plans that you will need to believe you can, and you will need to put in the time and effort. When you have a well thought out strategy, you will be miles ahead. Just having a plan is nothing without the action behind it, though. Your actions, day by day, one step at a time, will be the key to your brand new future. It would do you no good to have a great plan and no action.

What you get by achieving your goals is not as important as what you become by achieving your goals.

- Zig Ziglar

Goals

This chapter is called Mapping It Out because that's precisely what we are going to do. We are going to start with this dream that you have now checked with your life attributes. It's your dream, and it's something that you want to accomplish. Now we are going to take the dream and turn it into a goal. How do we do that?

In the previous chapter, I said, "you have figured out where you are starting from, and you have an understanding of where you want to go." You now have that understanding, but not the whole target, or the entire picture.

The translation of a dream into a goal requires adding a couple of other critical items. We have already checked it against our life attributes. Now, you are going to identify the 'why' you want this goal.

Is it because of what we will feel when we do it? Perhaps it is what we will think of ourselves? Another popular reason is that achieving a big dream stuffs it in someone else's face. There are tons of motives, but the underlying one that surrounds it all is that we will feel better in some way. What is that way? Be honest with yourself.

Before we move on, we need to have a quick chat about your' get back' motives. If you would like to pull up outside the place you work in some fancy car just to 'show them,' stop a moment. What would that do? For a very brief moment, you would experience one-upmanship. "I sure showed them!"

Did you? How hard did you work? How many hours did you plan and produce the action needed for you to have your fifteen seconds of nose rubbing? In the end, you have a nice car, sure, but the feelings of that one moment will fade fast. Instead of them hating you for the rest of their lives, they will forget you, and you worked so hard for nothing. When we break it all down, you were working for them, only from a different angle. You had to work hard to impress them with your success instead of just enjoying something else, something that you REALLY wanted for you or your family. Keep this in mind.

A goal is a dream with a deadline.

- Napoleon Hill

Now we are going to wrap your dreams with some dates.

Because of Purpose

You need to have a start date. A start date, oddly enough, is imperative. It may seem strange that you would have to set a start date. It is the commitment that you are making to yourself, and to others, that says I am going to begin working hard to accomplishing my goal starting on (insert date). That is your start date.

There are a couple of critical pieces of information that are necessary to finalize your goal. One of them is the end date, or the target date, or the due date as I like to call it. The due date is pretty simple. When do I want to have this by?

Sometimes, you have to set the due date before you build the plan because timing dictates it. As an example, let's say you are saving up for a big trip somewhere.

My wife and I went to Ireland a few years ago. We wanted to go during the first two weeks of May. We wanted to go at that time of year because we knew the weather was going to be at its best, or we would have to wait until the fall. It wasn't going to be too hot, and it wasn't going to be too cold. It was glorious weather.

It was spring, and everything was bright green. The weather was perfect for traveling around. Lows in the 50s with highs not quite reaching 75. It was awesome being there in the spring.

That goal was about timing. There were things that I had to do with the plan to complete it in the tight space that I had. In the end, it was worth the extra effort and sweat for that ten-day excursion, driving ourselves across Ireland. While we only got through a fraction of it, we fell in love with the people and the country.

Sometimes the due date becomes the most important thing. In that case, you build the plan between the start date and the due date.

Many a false step was made by standing still.

- Fortune Cookie

Most of the time, when you are defining your goal, the due date can be determined after you have developed your plan. You figure out all the things necessary to make this happen. Then you set the target date.

Sometimes it's a lot easier after you have your plan laid out to determine your due date. You might have thought it was going to take you six months to do something, but the plan looks more like ten months. It might be more work than you thought it was going to be, or there might be somethings you need to learn to complete it. As you develop your plans, be aware of points like this where you need to do some research and ask questions. Make sure you have built into your plan, or even ahead of time, places to gain that knowledge.

Give yourself a realistic amount of time to complete the plan, but never give yourself too much time. That is death to your goal. If you give yourself too much time, you're going to take all that time, and a little more.

I gave myself a timeframe for writing this book. I gave myself a little extra room because I wasn't sure how well the book was going to come together. I didn't know how many countless hours I was going to need sitting in my office in front of my laptop, staring at a blank screen.

My passion for teaching, sharing, and educating has kicked in full steam, and this is driving me to the finish line. At the time I am writing this chapter, I am fifteen days ahead of schedule. Because of that, I am going to take some time this weekend with the plan and make some adjustments to pull in my due date.

I am going to shorten my plan timeframe. That due date is one of those factors that can motivate you. It is staring at you. You can see it in the rearview mirror. If it is getting too close, hammer down with a little more effort.

Between your life attributes and your due date, you should have plenty of motivation to keep going, to keep pushing, to keep trying harder, until you reach your goal. Don't forget that you have the description of your dream to read for that little extra boost.

Now, let's start building the plan.

Action is the foundational key to all success.

- Pablo Picasso

Milestones

Today, many of you might be familiar with the term milestone. It started during the ancient Roman Empire when stones would be set up and carved, showing the distance between cities and then the distance from Rome.

The goal you are going to plan for needs a roadmap. This section and the next two sections are going to talk about building that roadmap. Much like a trip, you are going to have milestones. Today we call them mile markers, mileposts, kilometer plates, or other titles based on where you are in the world.

In our plans, a milestone represents a significant accomplishment and a larger portion of the overall plan. If we look at the driving trip we have been discussing, the one from Seattle to Miami, you could break it up using different milestones. One plan could have the trip broken down into individual days while a different planning pattern might break it down by states. It is up to you to decide which fits you or the situation the best.

One thing that you need to understand about milestones is that they do not have to happen sequentially. That is, they do not have to occur in order, one right after the other. You can be working on several different things at the same time. This is the difference between a linear plan and a parallel plan.

A linear plan is one that has all of the steps, tasks, and milestones set up so that you work one right after the other. This might be needed in a plan where you are building up your finances one piece at a time and then purchasing something for the overall goal. You would save up your money until you had enough to buy the first thing, then buy it, and move to the next step in your plan of saving for the next purchase. You would accomplish your milestones one at a time.

In a parallel plan, you would set things up so that you could work on different aspects of the plan at the same time. Let's say you wanted to take a trip to a country and wanted to learn some of the language first. You would work on the finances and planning of the trip at the same time as learning the language. Milestones would be accomplished together, instead of one at a time.

Neither one has any advantages over the other. The plan type to use is based on how things should and can happen as you move toward your goal.

As an example of planning out your milestones, let's look at planning an adventure trip. You would look at it and decide what the big pieces that have to occur are. The first one is money. You need to save up the money to be able to go on the trip. You will need airline flights to and from your particular destination. There is the car rental, overnight accommodations, and the things that you want to see and do. Finally, passports if you are headed out of the country. Each one of these become a milestone.

As mentioned, you can be working on one milestone path while you are working on another. In this example, saving the money for the trip can happen while you are doing some of the other things. You can be looking up and planning for the attractions you want to see AND working on gathering the money for the trip at the same time. As the money comes in, you would make a reservation for something, say the airline tickets, and then go back to saving. In this example, you can see that portions of the plan are happening in parallel while others are happening in a series or in a linear fashion.

Creating your plan will also help you see things that you might miss. In the above example, you need to plan for the attractions you want to see before you make plans for your overnight accommodations. Until you know what you what to do, you can't make a proper decision about where to stay for the night.

Once you have the major milestones figured out and written down, then you can move on to the next step of planning your goal.

It's a cinch by the inch, but hard by the yard.

- Unknown

Tasks

A goal is a big thing. When you look at it, you see one giant mountain of unknowns. It is very intimidating. Trust me, I know because I've been there. Writing this book is one of those massive mountains of a goal.

Taking your goal and slicing it down into milestones helps. It can seem a little more manageable, but those are still huge chunks. Basically, we have taken a giant mountain and pieced it out into hills. We will now continue to do this by examining our milestones and see the tasks within each.

Some beautiful things occur when we do this. One is that we take the opportunity to look at each milestone individually. With this focus, seeing the milestone as a single thing instead of one piece of a giant mass, it can become a little smaller in our eyes. You will see how that milestone can be accomplished by creating the tasks needed to complete it.

When we break down milestones into smaller sections, it is more controllable. As the quote on the previous page said, if we look at something as a yard, it is a long distance. If we break it down into smaller pieces, like inches, then it is simpler. Consider this step in the planning process breaking your plan into feet. The next step breaks it down into inches.

I enjoy podcasts and listen to several weekly that all deal with success in life. I heard a story about a man that spent time in a monastery in New York. He was cut off from everything for several weeks. The first night he was there, the monks had catered a dinner for a group and they asked him to wash some dishes. Of course, he agreed, not knowing that the group was five hundred people.

When they wheeled the cart of dishes, piled as high as the eye could see, he was floored. He told the monk that there was no way he could wash five hundred dishes. What the monk told him is a perfect revelation for what we are doing here.

The monk told him not to wash five hundred dishes, but instead to wash the one dish in his hand, and repeat that five hundred times.

Look at each of your milestones and take them apart into smaller tasks.

Steps

Have you ever heard the phrase that good things come in threes?

Without sounding too repetitive, we are now going to look at each task and break it down into yet smaller pieces called steps. Steps are the things that need to be done but laid out in its lowest form or something that might be done in one day. It is the steps that the above quote called an inch. "It's a cinch by the inch, but hard by the yard."

> # Great things are done by a series of small things brought together.
>
> ## - Vincent Van Gogh

You might be wondering why we would want to break the pathway to our goals into such small pieces. You have likely heard about those mammoth size steaks where people attempt to eat them in one sitting. If they can do it, the meal is on the house. When asked how the winners can do it, they always say something like one bite at a time.

With a goal, it is the same thing. When you can break down the path to your goal into small pieces, you will find the going a lot easier. Why would that be? It doesn't change how you get there, does it?

The answer is, of course, no. It doesn't change how you do it or in how much time it takes you to accomplish your dream. So why do it?

There are good reasons for this. One is that you can see certain areas where something might go wrong. When your plan is based on a tight timeline, you need to know where the trouble spots might occur before they happen. If you are headed out of the country, you need to make sure that you either have passports if you don't have them already, or if they are close to expiring, that you have enough time to get new ones.

Having the opportunity to see these hot spots in advance gives you the extra time to plan them out better or differently. You can also take advantage of the time you do have to move on them sooner rather than later.

As you are planning, you might find that there is something that you need to learn to accomplish your plan. Now you know that from the beginning, and you can start to learn it now or find someone to help you with that step or task.

Breaking your plan into steps gives you the satisfaction of checking things off on your plan as you continue being consistent and faithful to your dreams. As I am writing this book, I am marking off each section that I write as I move along. There is a big lift when you get to cross something off the list. Celebrate each win along the way. This can also help you keep your motivation up.

Finally, when you look at a small step, it can help to ease some of the anxiety you might have about the task. One thing to realize is achieving that which you have never had or done will require you to step out of your comfort zone. If the step is small, it will be easier to tackle. You will still have to get out there and make it happen, but the amount to accomplish is lighter. Once it is done, it will give you a confidence boost when you check it off from your list.

Taking things down to this level can help you troubleshoot your plan even before you begin and give you the encouragement you need along the way.

Be aware that small goals might not need tasks, just milestones and steps. Some areas of your plan might need tasks, and others might not. Be flexible with this based on the size of your goal and your plan.

Avoiding Overwhelmed

Some people thrive on having everything laid out in advance. They know what is going to happen not only today, but four months from now. Knowing this assures them for the future.

Others might become overwhelmed by looking at a long list of steps that need to be done. The volume of the to-dos feels like a heavy burden, and they can lose heart. Thankfully, there is a solution to this.

Break your down your goal into milestones. Then, either plan out the tasks now or jot down some notes about the tasks so you will remember them for later. Pull out your first milestone, write down the tasks, and then break down the first few tasks into steps. One of your steps before you reach the end of your list, should be to work on planning the next task, breaking it down into steps, so you have them ahead of time and will not lose your momentum.

Looking ahead forty-five to sixty days is usually a good target. As you are planning out your steps, stop at sixty days into the future and begin to complete the steps you have planned out immediately.

DO WANT YOU NEED TO DO SO THAT NOTHING STANDS IN THE WAY OF YOUR FUTURE.

Start Where You Are

For a lot of people, they haven't chased their dreams before. They have not felt the victory that comes from accomplishing something grand.

One thing that you can do for yourself is to start with what I like to call the instant win. I love the instant win for new chasers because they can get the feeling of success quickly. Being able to harness the emotions is critical to achieving success.

Let's use an example, and you can see how this all fits together. We are going to look at someone who is looking to drop some pounds and lower their A1C, which is the lab test used to determine if someone has diabetes.

Let's look at the goal. The goal could be a specific number of pounds to lose or a BMI range to attain. I would suggest that the goal not be something like 'be health' or 'get healthier.' There is nothing that will tell you exactly when you have achieved your goal. It must be measurable.

So, let's break this down into three milestones like this:

1. Create new healthy habits
2. Lose 50 pounds
3. Reduce A1C to 6.0

These will serve as a good example. Not only does it have the weight goal as a milestone, but there is something that must be learned, new healthy habits. The third milestone is a byproduct of both the new healthy habits and the reduction in weight. This will be a parallel plan, as all items will be worked at the same time.

The next thing to do is to break down your milestones into task sized accomplishments. Let's attack the first one, new healthy habits. You likely know what you need to do for each of your goals in life, and anything you don't know, you can quickly learn about by finding expert advice on the internet, reading books, or asking friends. Under the milestone Create New Healthy Habits, you might have:

A. Eliminate sugar
B. Learn 50 new healthy recipes
C. Exercise 5 times a week

Here is where you want to find an instant win. For Eliminate Sugar, you might try changing out a snack for something better or tossing a bag of chips into the trash. It needs to be something that you can get behind and enjoy the emotion of crossing off a step from your list.

For Exercise, you might try walking one mile. Even though it sounds like a lot, it is only 2000 steps on average. It's a little bigger than the snack so that it would be a step up. This would make a great second win.

The idea is to have measurable goals across everything you do. Each one here can be measured in some way. Your cell phone can have an app that will measure your steps, tossing out the bag of chips is easily measured, and you will know when you change out a snack.

Get some quick wins to get you started on the journey to your goal.

Taking Action

There it is. You have everything written out and planned to the best of your ability. You have a goal, dates, and reasons. You double-checked to make sure this is your goal and that you are totally on board with it.

You have your milestones, they are broken out into tasks, and they are broken down into steps. You have seen some potential problem areas and built your plan to accommodate for that. There is only one thing left.

Yes, we need to talk about it. That great gray beast is in the house. It isn't going anywhere, so we might as well deal with it right now, being the people of action that we are. Let's address the elephant in the room. His name is Action.

Because of Purpose

ACTIONS PRODUCE RESULTS. NOTHING ELSE WILL.

No matter what you hear, nothing takes the place of action. You can want, wish, and hope all you want, but you MUST take action.

If you don't move forward, you will not move forward. You must produce action, and you have to complete the steps. No one will do it for you. It is up to you.

There are a few reasons that people hesitate to produce activity toward their dreams. Doubt is a big one.

"What if it doesn't work?"

If you try something and it doesn't work, then take a look at the situation and consider something for a moment. How many times have you tried something like this before? This is likely your first time. Why? Because, this is the first time you have attempted to reach for your goals.

Do not beat yourself up over anything. You are in uncharted waters. This is new, and you will likely slip a few times getting up the hill. It happens. Everyone who works for their dreams has had something go sideways or not hit the mark perfectly every time.

FAILURE IS AN OPTION, BUT GIVING UP IS NOT.

It took Thomas Edison ten thousand times to get the light bulb right. Imagine that. Ten thousand electric light bulbs didn't work out. He just continued to work his plan and did it.

"What if I have to replan everything completely?"

Because of Purpose

Then welcome to the club where the price of admission is to retool the path to your future. There have been plenty of times I have had to, and thousands of people like us. They created their new plan, and their future was the bright and shining star they dreamt it would be.

If you run into issues, and you see that your plan is not going to work, then, by all means, rework your plan and jump back in. Do not stop. Never give up. It is a time to learn and see things from a more educated place. Nelson Mandela said, "I never lose. I either win or I learn." Here is your chance to learn and then win.

"I don't think I can do it."

You are not alone. When we step out to do something, to achieve that which we have never done, there will be some butterflies. Expect it so that when it does happen, you already knew they were coming.

Self-doubt can be an issue, particularly when you are starting out for the first time. That is one of the reasons it's best to use smaller goals to start.

When you doubt, but do it anyway, you will find that your file cabinet will begin to change. What is stored in your history will change. Having done something that you doubted before, but did it anyway, will arm you with the courage to try something else.

I wish I could tell you that having a great plan will answer every question and remove all the uncertainty you may have. That isn't the case. What is true is that action wins out overall. You have no greater ability than this; to go out there and do it anyway.

Sever self-doubt with the sword of action.

- Vann Lantz

Risk is a part of everyday life. Just driving to work is a risk. We put our seat belts on to help mitigate some of that risk. We drive defensively to help offset some of the hazards. We have lights and windshield wipers at the ready. Each one of these tools is there, prepared to address the dangers. When we do this, it is called a calculated risk.

A calculated risk is when we lessen or ease the dangers of what we are going to do. You put on a seat belt not so you will have an accident, but in case you do, you will be protected. You don't drive around with your wipers going all the time, just when it rains.

All courses of action are risky,
so prudence is not in avoiding danger
(it's impossible), but calculating risk
and acting decisively.
Make mistakes of ambition and not
mistakes of sloth.
Develop the strengths to do bold
things, not the strength to suffer.

- Niccolo Machiavelli

Because of Purpose

Chapter 7

Walking Your Path

Your Reason

Within every goal, no matter how perfectly planned or aligned it is to your life attributes, there must be a reason. It is this reason which is a big part of the motivation that will help you to go for the next step when you get down. Each time you want to quit or give up, your reason will push you through.

For each goal, ask yourself, what is the reason. Why do you want it?

This next exercise might be a little uncomfortable. You will need to answer some potentially hard questions honestly. Dig deep within yourself.

Select one of your goals. Why do you want it? Don't just nod at the question. Formulate a real answer. There are a lot of reasons why, but what is your reason for that one goal?

Once you have your reason written done, look at it again. We are going to shake down your answer.

If your goal is to have a fast car, what was your reason?

"To drive fast!"

That is not a real reason. Keep digging.

"Because it's cool, and I've always wanted one."

OK, hold on to the part about wanting one. Let's focus on the cool part of your answer. Why? Why is it cool?

"Because it's a cool car, it's a hypercar."

Again, why is this your goal? You might be disappointed with your real answer.

"Because I'll be the only one of my friends to have one, and I can pull up in it in front of the guys at work who thought little of me."

There are good reasons, and then there are not so good reasons. Revenge or 'upmanship' is not usually a good reason. The problem with that as your reason is you are placing your efforts, your drive, and your money on someone else's hook. Don't fall victim to this.

Now, if your reason is more along the lines of, "I've wanted one since I was eight, and this is the exact car I've been dreaming of since then." We might have something now. This is the type of drive you need to have.

When you are completing your "reason" exercise, make sure you ask yourself why at least three times. Get real with yourself in this. Your reason is going to be a part of the driving force you will need to complete your journey to this goal.

Sometimes, when you look at your plan and your reason, you might decide that the reason just isn't strong enough to stick with it. It might be that you decide your plan is too much work for the size of your reason. You will learn a lot about your dreams working through your reasons why.

One of the things that will help you immensely is to develop an emotional attachment to your goal. You need a desire and a passion for your purpose. Let's try a different angle on the car.

You must be hungry.
Whatever you want in life, you must be hungry. If you're not hungry, you'll never be successful. So you always have to be hungry for what you want.
- Jason Diesel

"I want a nice sporty four-door car." Yes, they make them.

Great. Why?

"We need the extra room with the kids/grandkids getting older. Our current car doesn't work for us anymore."

You are doing good so far. Why?

"When we bought our current car, it was the best we could do at the time. It's too small, and we want to do some driving vacations."

Keep going. Why?

"Because time with my family is the most important thing to me. They are getting older and will be off to seek their own journey soon. Time is getting short."

Time with the family and the realization that time is getting short with them. With that, you can build a dream. This is the type of reason that can keep you pushing through until you accomplish your goal.

The Journey is the Goal

I am about to blow your mind. Make sure you read and understand this section before moving on to the rest of the book. The goal is not the goal, but merely the reward at the end of a journey.

Say what? But you said...

Don't get me wrong or misunderstand what I am saying. The goal is incredible! We aim for the goal, and that is our direction. Something magical happens on our way to the dreams of our life.

If you decided to run a marathon, you wouldn't just sign up and take off. You would put in the time and effort to work out, to train in running, building your abilities and stamina as you went along. Nutrition would be something to learn so you could adequately fuel up. You would set smaller goals along the way and work to accomplish them.

When you got to the starting line, would you be the same person you were months earlier?

As we take our journey to complete our goals, something happens to us. We become someone better than when we started. Something I read once talked about a person who decided to run an ultra marathon. This is twice the distance of a marathon all run at once.

They said something that stuck with me. They wanted to know who they would need to be to run an ultramarathon, and they were interested in meeting that person.

TO ACCOMPLISH YOUR GOALS, WHO DO YOU NEED TO BECOME, OR BETTER PUT, WHAT THINGS DO YOU NEED TO LEARN AND CHANGE WITHIN YOURSELF?

What habits do you need to pick up and which ones do you need to leave by the roadside?

Ask anyone who has finished a big goal, and question them about the changes in their lives. They will be able to tell you about the incredible changes they made. It is all part of the journey.

Your future is going to need something more than you have been in the past. Why? Because you are going to have more and do more than you ever had. Therefore, you will need to be more. You might need more courage to accomplish some of your tasks. It might be money management, creativity, or business knowledge.

So, when I say that the journey is the goal, you can understand it in a better light. The journey includes the things you will learn, the new habits or traits you pick up, and the enjoyment of the climb to the top.

Enjoy, better yet, embrace the inner you, the one that has been there all the time. It's about time you got to know each other better.

Keeping Focused

Staying on track can be tough at times. We run hard and like to take breaks. Sometimes we can lose our momentum, which equals losing our motivation. If that happens, you will have a battle to get back to it.

Use your plan to your best advantage. Not only can it tell you what the next step is, but many folks assign dates to milestones and even tasks. If you have a deadline staring you down, you know you need to get busy. Use your plan to hold yourself accountable. If you see things are piling up, get busy.

Do what you have to do today so you can do what you want to tomorrow.

- Keith Whitaker from the YouTube channel Sailing Zatara

This is not to say that you can't take a moment. Tonight, my wife and I spent some quality, quiet time together. Knowing my plan and that I am ahead of schedule, I could take that time without worry or any anxiety. I wasn't thinking about my next section to write or the upcoming deadlines. I wiped that from my mind, which is easy to do when you are on schedule or ahead of schedule.

One thing that a lot of successful people do is to develop an accountability group or an accountability partner. This is when like-minded people hold each other to what they say they are going to do. For instance, if you told your accountability partner that you would have something done by a specific date, then when you spoke next, they would bring it up and see if you were true to your word.

Another option is to have a life coach. Here is more than an accountability partner. A life coach is a person who can walk you through the entire process from start to finish. They not only hold you to your word, but they can help you dig down into your goal, help you flesh out your plan, and more. By the time this book has been released, *Because of Purpose* will have a life coach system coming soon. If you are interested, consult our web site for more information.

Ways to Motivate Yourself

Motivation never seems to last for long, but that's OK. There are so many ways you can rekindle your motivation. Begin each day by stoking your motivation. If your motivation wanes, you'll know how to give it a big boost.

Some people seem to be motivated all of the time. This isn't just a random phenomenon. They instinctively know how to drive themselves to success. For the rest of us that aren't so lucky, we can learn.

I have mentioned several tools you can use to keep or increase your motivation. Let's recap them and add several more to your list of available resources to keep you fired up.

Promise Yourself A Reward For Completing A Task Or A Milestone

Give yourself something to look forward to! It could be something as a meal out. Maybe you'll give yourself a quick TV break. It just needs to be something that will help you along. If you complete a significant milestone, how about a short weekend trip out of town or a little something from your favorite store?

> **People often say that motivation doesn't last. Well, neither does bathing – that's why we recommend it daily.**
>
> **- Zig Ziglar**

Revisit Your Reason Why And The Emotion

Go back to your plan and kindle again the flame. Think about the feeling you will have when you accomplish the goal. Focus on the emotions that we talked about at the beginning of this chapter.

List The Advantages Of Completing It

It could be a milestone or even a step. If you lack a little drive, then ask yourself, what are the advantages of getting your task completed? What benefits do you receive? Remind yourself of what you're getting out of the deal. Go back to your goal and look at the life attributes that match this goal.

List The Disadvantages Of Not Completing It

Sometimes, disadvantages can be even more potent than advantages. Use pain to your advantage. What are the penalties of not getting it done? How will you suffer? What are the negative consequences? You can gain a lot of motivation by recognizing the advantages and disadvantages of taking, or not taking, an action.

Read Your Dream Description

Remember that detailed description that you made back in chapter five? Pull it out. Don't just read it, live it. Close your eyes and envision it happening. Live in that moment.

Tackle It Anyway

Sometimes you just need to get to work. You would be surprised how many times getting back in the groove is as simple as just getting back out there.

Watch An Inspirational Video

I give this with a word of caution. Set a time limit. Don't get too carried away and blow a lot of time. Sometimes I will watch a talk by Tim Han from Success Insiders or something from Mike Rayburn. Other times, I will watch a video about my goal. It could be someone doing what I want or talking about what I aim to have.

Music!

I am a huge music fan and have found some good uplifting music out there. You would be surprised where it will pop up. It might be a small part of a verse or maybe the chorus that hits you.

Most of all...

Tomorrow becomes never. No matter how small the task, take the first step now!

- Timothy Ferris

Chapter 8

Daily Habits

Let's talk about making some choices in your life, and we will start with your morning routine.

What, a touchy subject? Good. I like to stir the pot. It keeps life interesting. HA!

Your Morning Routine

Seriously though, we do need to talk about your mornings. Like most folks, your morning routine is crammed with too much to do and not enough time to do it. If you have kids, that only adds…no, it multiplies it. I have two adult children, so I've been there.

Why are mornings so blasted hard? Mostly due to self-sabotage, I hate to admit it. I would set my alarm for a time that was a little behind where it should have been. Then, when the alarm went off, I would turn it off and lay there. I didn't want to get up. Who wants to get up anyway?

Because of Purpose

Once I did make it out of bed, it took a bit to get moving. I would get dressed quickly because I laid there too long, eat breakfast, and fire myself out the door only to face the traffic I hated so much. Why? Because they were so grumpy. Of course, they were. They didn't want to be up either.

Mornings just weren't my thing. I had a motto. "There is no such thing as a good morning until about 11 because then it's not really morning anymore."

I was kind of defeated before I even got up.

Do you know what you are telling yourself and the world with that kind of a morning? That you do not want to be up, and that you don't want to start your day. That is the vibe you are putting off.

I am not going to promise you that you will instantly become a morning person, or even that you will finally be one. For so many years, I HAD to get up early. It sucked. The alarm clock, or as I called it, the leash, would go off, and I would just lay there, trying to bask in as much time in bed as I could.

After introducing my morning routine with the great things it has to offer, starting my morning on a high note, I loved it. I might still prefer to be a late morning person, but I will NOT change my morning routine one bit. I get more things done before by 8 AM than most people do all day at work. Now, I am going to show you how to start your day off in the right way.

The first thing you need to do is to make a choice that you will do whatever it takes to start out each day the best way possible, even if it means getting up a little earlier. Yes, earlier. Trust me. You won't die from it. In fact, you might feel like you got your life back, or have it under control for the first time.

I am about to introduce four simple things that will start you in the right direction every morning. They are so vital to the rest of your life that you need to make room for them. They are Targeting, Gas in Your Tank, Seeing Your Future, and Waking Up the Person Inside.

You might be wondering how much time do I need to make room for, and why does it need to be in the morning?

The time of day is easy. If you were to do these at the end of the day, you would find that your mind is tired. Your mind and body are already headed to bed. Your focus and concentration are gone.

The middle of the day is not right, either at lunch or after dinner. Your mind is already racing with a thousand other things. There are distractions at work and on the TV.

With the morning, you can create the time easily, and you have the added benefit that you will affect your mind and your thoughts for the rest of the day. Starting your day out the right way creates momentum. You got off to a great start, and now you are ready.

When it comes to the amount of time, it is always a personal choice, but thirty to forty minutes is a superb start. My morning routine runs about an hour to an hour and a half, but there are some explanations needed to understand it. More about that later.

If you aren't happy with the way things are in your life, remember this. You are where you are because of the choices you have made and the choices you haven't made. It might be time for some new choices.

> Your life is a result of the choices you make. If you don't like your life, it's time to start making different choices.
>
> - Unknown

Targeting

When you wake up, grab a pen and paper and start writing. Targeting is about focusing your thoughts for the day. A few minutes of some straightforward journaling will help you with this.

Targeting is not about writing a diary, attempting to capture what happened yesterday. It doesn't matter what fool cut you off in traffic or that nasty thing that person at work said to you. The goal for targeting is to focus your thoughts on the day ahead of you. First thing in the morning is the best time for this because your mind is fresh and not bogged down with the day yet.

Scan your mind for thoughts and ideas. Write down anything that can help you with a situation you have, something that might get you closer to your goal, or ideas for pondering on later. Some mornings you may not have anything. That's fine. Just be ready every morning.

Also, jot down a few things that you are grateful for in your life. You don't need a lot. A couple will do. By doing this, you will start your day with gratitude on your mind and in your heart. Focus on each one for a minute and let the gratefulness come to the surface. No matter where you are in life or situation, you can always find something to be grateful for.

Spend five to ten minutes journaling.

Waking Up the Person Inside

Now that the person on the outside is awake let's wake up the person on the inside.

Everyone has the potential to become whatever they want or accomplish anything they can conceive. It is true. If you have been doing everything in the book up to now, you have found out what makes you tick, you have a clear goal written down, and you have a beautiful plan drawn out. Have you ever had that before? If you are like a lot of people, you have not.

These are significant steps towards achieving what you have been dreaming about. You are discovering that your potential is alive.

Look back at chapter three. We talked about the mind. Remember the filing cabinet? I told you that I was going to show you a way to fill your file cabinet with good beliefs. With enough goodness, it can overcome the bad.

This is about rewiring or reprogramming your mind. You have been taught to think about things in one way. Now, by putting new information in your file cabinet, you are training your brain to think differently than it has before.

"You believe yourself the most." You may have heard this phrase before, or something like it. In this single phrase, you may find the answer to the thing that is holding you back. What do you say to yourself when something goes wrong? Probably something negative. What about when something goes right? "That was luck" or some other comment that washes away anything positive? You are not alone.

Because of Purpose

Every day we are bombarded with stuff that drags us down. People have said hurtful things to us in the past. We hear others complaining about something, someone insults another person, and I won't even start with the barrage of stuff on the news. It is no wonder we say negative things to ourselves.

Now, you have a grand opportunity not only to counterbalance all of that but to create the life you want so you can live the life you dream about. Welcome to the magnificent world of affirmations. It's time to fill your filing cabinet with good stuff about you.

You cannot create the income, impact, and life you're capable of until you master your mindset. The moment you master your mindset, everything changes.

- Tim Han

Here are a few things to understand about affirmations before we move on. Affirmation statements have been studied and proven that they do work. In one study done at Carnegie Mellon University, they found that self-affirmation statements can positively affect outcomes in someone's life.

David Creswell is an assistant professor of Psychology at the University. He said, "An emerging set of published studies suggest that a brief self-affirmation activity at the beginning of a school term can boost academic grade-point averages in underperforming kids."

In the summer of 2013, Carnegie Mellon University did a study on self-affirmations. They had college students complete a problem-solving task under a time pressure. They broke things down into three groups. The first was those not under chronic high stress in their daily life, which we will call the low-stress group. The second was those under chronic high stress. The second group was divided into two groups. One half they had take the test as is, while the other half did the test after reciting some affirmations.

The low-stress group set the baseline. In the high-stress group, those that didn't recite the affirmations did approximately 50% worse than those in the low-stress group. Those high-stress folks who did the affirmations did as well as those in the low-stress group.

Now, imagine what would happen if you did affirmations as a matter of course in your life! You would continue to improve and gain the victory of your dreams in the process.

An affirmation statement is not lying to yourself. It is actually telling yourself the truth, and possibly for the first time. Affirmations give you a blank canvas for allowing you to shift your thoughts to what can be.

Let me say this. Affirmations are about bringing what you can do to the surface. This is not a 'blab it and grab it' situation. Stating an affirmation that says you have muscles as big as Arnold Schwarzenegger for three weeks will do absolutely nothing for you. If you want big muscles, then your affirmations need to be along the lines of 'I enjoy working out' or 'when I work out, I give it everything I have.'

Because of Purpose

It's the same way with money and big houses. Just saying it does nothing for you. Your affirmation program should be built on how you, as a person, need to be to accomplish your goals.

One of the things that I have worked on is acting immediately on something that needs to be done, versus putting it off. One of the affirmations I used was, "I am a man of action. I easily motivate myself to do anything that needs to be done."

Affirmations are more about becoming the person you need to be. While they focus on the future, they are written in the present. Saying something like, "I will become a man of action" is future tense. This is one of those situations where tomorrow never comes. 'I will' is at some distant point in the unknown future. Avoid this when creating your affirmations.

They need to be positive. Focus on what you want to be, not what you don't want to be. The phrase "I will not be a procrastinator" or "I am not lazy" doesn't cut it. It is directly addressing the negative in your life, which is what we are trying to get rid of. Your brain knows you are saying you will not be lazy because you are lazy. The more you talk about it, the more you are focusing on it. It's like telling someone not to think about a particular object and guaranteed, that's all they can think about.

Remember when we talked about the file cabinet in our minds? The only way to get rid of the negative stuff in there is to begin filling your cabinet with all the good things about you. There is no flush button. You have to put positive things in to push out the garbage that you have been told and believed for all of these years.

One thing that I like to do is use quotes that I like from other people I respect and turn them into affirmations. When one rings with me, I want to harness that emotional connection.

Timothy Ferris made a statement that spoke to me. "Tomorrow becomes never. No matter how small the task, take the first step now!" I changed this into the affirmation of "No matter how small the task, I always take the first step now!"

Affirmations should be personal, now, and positive. Don't have too many. Select a few topics, back them up with several declarations each, and write them down. Then, when you are ready to read your statements, you have them all in one spot.

One last thing on affirmation statements is to read them, hopefully out loud, but read them with intense emotion. Read it like it means something to you because it does. This is all about your future. Get excited and get fired up.

Take five minutes to say your affirmations.

Seeing Your Future

Ask any athlete what they do just before they perform. They will tell you that they envision winning. Runners will tell you that they have run the race many times long before they set foot on the track. This is called visualization.

Just like your affirmation statements help you to gear up for life, visualization is what I like to call the movie version of the book. Having just completed my affirmations, I take the time to visualize a particular situation. It could be something that I need to do during the day, or the joy of having completed a milestone or a goal I have been working to achieve.

When you visualize, be detailed. Where are you? What is the weather? Who else is there? What are you wearing? The more accurate you get, the more your mind accepts it not as just a fanciful wish but a picture into your future.

Perform your visualizations for five minutes or so.

Gas in Your Tank

We all know what happens if we don't have any gas in our vehicle. It stops working. It is an easy concept to understand. Your car takes fuel to run the engine, and if you run out, you come to a stop.

The best way to keep yourself pumped, pardon the pun, is to take in good material regularly. Each day, you should be reading self-help or personal productivity books. For some people, this sounds like a drag. "I don't like to read." I can hear it now, but only because I was one of those people.

If it wasn't work-related, I didn't have time for it. The truth was, I just didn't like reading. Well, that has changed. Now, I look forward to reading. In that book I'm holding, I might find something that will trigger a thought or give me a new realization about life, success, or me. I want every advantage I can get. So do you, which is why you are reading this book right now.

On our website, you will find a great list of books to get you started on your way. After you have read several books, you might find that you like specific authors or topics better than others. Great. Use that to your advantage.

Another thing I do, and I say that this is in addition to, not in replacement of, is audiobooks. When my wife and I go somewhere, you can often find us listening to an audiobook on something. It is fascinating, I feel, when the author reads their own book. You get to hear their emphasis and emotions in specific sentences that might not get read that way.

Many of the books that are linked on our website can be found in various audio retailers also. Don't let this be your only form of filling your tank. When you sit down and read something for yourself, you will retain more of it than listening to it. I use audiobooks as a supplement to reading.

Set aside twenty minutes for reading in the morning. This does not include additional reading or listening time you spend during the day.

Putting It All Together

The number one question I am asked about all of this is, "Will it work?" The answer is, "Absolutely!" It does work.

The other question is, "How much time is all of this going to take?" Here is how I would lay it out, especially if you are new to having a morning routine.

For targeting, the journaling you do to get your mind focused on the day ahead, I would set out about five to ten minutes.

For waking up the person inside, your affirmations, take no more than five minutes.

For seeing your future, visualizing your near or distant future, set aside about five minutes.

For putting gas in your tank, and I am just talking about reading first thing in the morning, take twenty minutes. You would be surprised how much reading you can do in twenty minutes. You will plow through a good number of books in a year.

Everything together, set aside around thirty-five to forty minutes each morning to complete your new morning routine. As you become accustomed to this, you might find you want to include other things in your morning. If this is the first time you have had a morning routine, give this a few weeks to set in before adding anything to it.

Because of Purpose

The first hour of the morning is the rudder of the day.

- Henry Ward Beecher

Chapter 9

Time, Money, and More

Time

One of the obstacles you will have to overcome is the statement we all have heard and even said many times before. "I just don't have the time." Let's talk about time.

Time Management

Managing your time is one of those things that people know they need to do but have no clue about doing it. How can you manage something that doesn't stay still and that you can't collect or purchase more of it? Guess what? We can't manage time.

Time is something that cannot be manhandled into doing what we want. The best we can do, and it is truly the best thing, is to manage ourselves.

Look at it this way. You can't manage the oceans or the air. They are there, and they will do precisely what they will. You can't stop a massive tsunami or a wind storm. They are going to happen, no matter what.

> # Time Management is really a misnomer – the challenge is not to manage time, but to manage ourselves.
>
> ## - Stephen Covey

You can manage yourself in those environments. You can get a boat, learn to swim, get a life jacket, and a ton of other things. You can also get on an airplane. Just as there are ways for you to work within those environments, you can learn to work within time.

Managing time is more about you, how you approach time than anything else.

Time Wasters

There are things out there that are great time wasters, but sometimes we don't see them. We might not even see them as wasting time. The first one that comes to mind, and you already know which one I am going to say, is television.

People use it to pass the time. Yes, the shows can be entertaining, but while you are watching that show, you aren't getting things done.

IF YOU DON'T GET THINGS DONE, YOU WILL NEVER MAKE IT TO LIVING YOUR DREAMS.

Let's look at a few more things that can help you redeem your time.

Goals, big goals, especially, require time. They also need commitment and focus. Try keeping a record of how you spend your time during the day. You will find things in your day that are not producing any results and can be curbed or cut out completely.

Time - an element of untold value, uncontrolled dimensions, and the currency of life that we can spend as we wish. Be careful how you spend it, for regret is not the same as reward, yet they cost the same.

- Vann Lantz

Surfing the internet can be a significant time consumer. Facebook and YouTube are both at the top of the list. If you are needed some instruction in something or a quick inspirational lift, then go for it. But stop quickly. There is no need to watch a parakeet dance the Samba.

With the invention of the smartphone has come many marvelous things. We communicate more and in different ways than ever before. It also has opened up a tidal wave of games to play. Those games won't put any extra time in your pocket.

Every moment you play, you lose time. There is no winning in life with those games, no matter what the score is.

I was a long time sufferer of procrastination. I could find a hundred ways to put off what needed to be done and always convince myself that I was going to do it later. Never put off what needs to be done. Do it now. Be a person of action and get things done.

Another one is seeking pleasure versus seeking progress. Pursuing those things that do nothing but make you feel good for a brief moment will take up the time you need to get to your goals. I'm not saying you shouldn't feel good every so often, but don't let those times become so frequent that you lose your focus. You will have plenty of time for them after you are living your dreams.

On that topic, progress comes from moving forward.

YOU CAN ONLY MOVE FORWARD IF YOUR WORK IS FOCUSED ON YOUR GOALS. BEING BUSY IS NOT SUCCESS; IT'S ONLY BEING BUSY.

Instead of making time to reach your dreams, you will be wasting time and will have little reward to show for it.

Creating Time

In today's era, we understand more and more how the hamster feels as he runs on his wheel. We get up, go to work, return home, eat dinner, watch TV, and then go to bed. Five or more times a week, this situation is played out in our lives. It seems like there isn't enough time for more things to do.

Let me ask you this. At your current progress, where will you be five years or even ten years from now? Unless things change, you know you will be no closer to living the life you want. You need to create time for the important stuff.

If you need to make time for something, make time for it. Don't make excuses about why you don't have time to do it.

- Jodie Dewberry

Create a to-do list each day. Write down the three MOST essential tasks you need to accomplish. Make sure at least one of them is in line with the current step of your plan. Let those three be your focus for the day. Anything else you get done that day is extra wins!

Shift your focus from perfection to progress. Get stuff done without worrying about the minor imperfections that might occur along to way. Each action you take on your plan pushes you toward your goals. Perfection can be an excuse to take too much time on a single thing. Get it done and then move on to the next important thing.

About midday, stop for a moment and examine how you are doing on your list. Are you focused on the three most important items? If not, change your focus and get back on track.

If you see something that needs to be done, add it to a list of additional to-do's. Don't stop your progress. Jot it down and get to it later, after your prioritized list.

A lot of times, you will hear people tell you to say "no" when people ask you to do something or help out. We want to be helpful and responsive to the needs of others, but there are times when we need to get our things done first. It will feel a little odd in the beginning, but you will find the clock pulling in your favor. You also won't be up at midnight baking cupcakes...again.

Money

Investing in YOU

When we invest in something, it is a process of taking something of value, typically money, and putting it into some investment or account that promises to return more money or value than what you began with.

You are an excellent place to invest. To invest in yourself means investing in your future. There are many ways to this. Books are a beautiful place to start. When you buy a book, you will need days or weeks to read it. Information is brought into your mind and will stay with you. When you want a refresh, read it again.

WHEN YOU INVEST IN YOURSELF, THIS IS SOMETHING THAT WILL ONLY INCREASE IN VALUE AS YOU PUT IT INTO MOTION.

Think about this book, *Because of Purpose*. You have learned your purpose in life, written down your dreams and goals, created plans to change your future, and now have yourself ready to put all of this into action.

> Investing in yourself is the best thing you can do. Anything that improves your own talents; nobody can tax it or take it away from you. They can run up huge deficits and the dollar can become worth far less. You can have all kinds of things happen. But if you've got talent yourself, and you've maximized your talent, you've got a tremendous asset that can return ten-fold.
>
> - Warren Buffett

    Be wise and prudent when you are spending your money, even when you are investing in yourself. It's easy to see something and think that it will make you better. You are as awesome as you need to be already; you just need to wake up that true inner self.

I'm not going to talk to you about brown-bagging your lunch versus eating out. This isn't about cutting your lunch and coffee fund to save money. If you can, and it will help you to achieve your dreams sooner, then, by all means, do that.

The point here is that you shouldn't run out and spend a lot of money all at once, thinking it is the answer or key to your future. You alone are that.

Downtime

Before we begin, let's define downtime, so we are all on the same page. In computer terms, downtime is when the computers aren't working. Typically, this is a bad thing. For us humans, downtime is when we are not working, but it's a good thing.

> **TAKING TIME FOR YOURSELF AND YOUR FAMILY IS AN ESSENTIAL PART OF LIFE.**

You need this break to recharge and refresh. It won't do you any good if you wear out before you can enjoy the fruits of your labor. Downtime can be anything from a simple short break of activities to a vacation.

So, let's look at the why, when, and how of personal downtime.

Why

Downtime can help prevent burnout. Burnout is when you are exhausted physically and mentally, having run out of steam. When this happens, things just aren't worth the effort, and nothing seems to work right, causing more stress.

When we begin a new something that we are excited about, we enter the happy phase, or you might call it the honeymoon phase. Things are terrific, we are enthusiastic about our project or goal, and we have the pedal to the metal.

Then starts the bumps in the road. They aren't always there, but they do happen. Something will pop up that, until recently, you could generally handle with all the grace and style of Gene Kelly dancing across the stage. Now, each issue seems bigger and more daunting than before.

Pretty soon, the potholes become a way of life. They are always there, or so it appears. You don't feel you are making any headway. This constant feeling of stress is noted with anger, consumption of extra amounts of caffeine, and even physical trouble.

Full-blown burnout is accompanied by behavioral changes, neglecting personal needs, and a constant pessimistic attitude.

If full-blown burnout continues, it hits critical mass. This is were things can get very dangerous. The ideal situation in all of this is to stop it before it gets this bad.

Having some downtime can help to prevent this progression from occurring. If you are having problems, as always, seek professional assistance.

As I have mentioned, there are consequences for pushing hard 100% of the time. If you think this sounds backward from everything I have been telling you so far, it really isn't. If you want to execute at your peak performance, you have to take some time for yourself. If you don't, your ability to work at your best will slide off.

When

The next piece of the puzzle is when to take a breather. You don't want to stop too often or for too long. This will cause your plan to get off track. So, how often is enough? I will show you a few things that I do, but you will need to find your stride for this. Just remember, there is a difference between resting so you can push hard and resting so you don't have to push hard.

I take time once a week, on Saturday, as a time off from most of my work. I still do my morning routine, and I will plan a few simple things to do that are goal-oriented, but most of the day, I rest or have fun with my family.

If a man cannot earn a living working six days a week, what would make him think he could make it if he works seven days a week?

- Truett Cathy

Another way to get some downtime is to have certain breaks in your plan. While I might celebrate a step that was hard or challenging in some way, I don't take downtime for something like that. I will take a break if a task was particularly difficult or if it took a while to finish, but not too often. Breaking the momentum is something that you don't want to do. Now when we start talking about the biggies, the milestones, I will take a break of a day. This break not only gives me time to celebrate and enjoy a moment but also I can look at my plan and begin to focus on the next task.

Now a goal deserves a rest and reset. Most of the time, I am so amped up from completing a goal I spend my downtime thinking about planning the next goal, but I try to resist. If your goal is a vacation, then you are all set. As soon as you finish your goal, pack your bags, and enjoy your time.

How

How people enjoy their downtime is as varied as the people themselves. The amount of time you rest and the amount of money you will spend is something that must be considered. You need the rest and should take the break, but spending too much cash that might be better put to use, is losing ground.

The main thing about downtime is to shut off and relax. I know some folks who will lock the doors, turn off the cell phones and computers, and call it a movie day. Others like to go for a walk in nature or take a drive somewhere.

It doesn't matter so much what you do, as long as you are rested and ready to get back to conquering your dreams when you are done.

What if, What if Not

So many questions plague our minds when we are trying to get ahead. What if this happens? What if that doesn't happen? It is a lot to consider.

Undoubtedly, you have heard the phrase that you are your own worst enemy, and you know what I am about to say next. It's true. We question everything in life that is new and different, even ourselves.

Because of Purpose

The problem is that we tend to believe our thoughts the most. We hear our voice the loudest. Most of the time, we aren't telling ourselves good things. It is a habit, and we do it a lot. If you could write down what you tell yourself during the day, you would understand how much you undermine yourself daily.

Some of the questions we ask ourselves can play a part in our undoing. We ask such harsh questions like, "Am I sure I know what I'm doing?" Sometimes the doubt comes in through statements such as, "This isn't right. It can't work." or "I don't think I can do this."

Everything we doubt comes down to fear. Fear is a stone-cold slap in our face each time it shows up. It attacks when we least expect it. The best way to counteract this is to say your affirmations at least once a day to help combat these thoughts. When the doubt creeps in, we can counter it with our affirmations and mentally and emotionally get things back on track.

Looking at fear, sometimes square in the face, we need to know why it is there and what it is trying to do within us. Being afraid of an unknown future, something that we have never experienced before, pushing our abilities, and what we think we are capable of, is all part of it.

Sometimes our fear is heard in the question, "What if I don't make it?"

As I have been, and will always be, I'm going to be completely honest with you. That is a possibility. If you set a big goal and a tight timeline, there is always the chance that you might not make it. So, what happens if you don't?

If you don't make your goal, the first thing you need to do it commit to moving forward no matter what. If you give up,

Because of Purpose

you lose all the ground you have covered. You have grown, stretched, and learned so much to get this far. Do not quit.

If you have made some distance, keep pushing on. It doesn't even matter how much. If you have pressed forward one step, quickly do another. Build momentum and get back into the journey.

Next, look at how far you have come and pat yourself on the back. The tasks you completed and the things you've learned only make you better. You are becoming the person you need to be to move forward into your dreams.

Finally, shut down the ney sayers. In your mind, shut them down. Do not allow them to drag you down. In the long run, they don't matter anyway. If they aren't saying anything, and most won't, don't worry about what they might be thinking.

And as for what you might be thinking, make sure it is in high-spirits and congratulatory. But most of all, don't stop in the pursuit of your dreams.

So be bold and don't worry about what people think.
They don't do it that often anyway.

- Timothy Ferriss

Because of Purpose

Chapter 10

An Interview with Paul A Jones

Paul Jones is an incredibly skilled artist, able to render paintings that rival photographs in realism and color. I had a chance to sit down with Paul to discuss his road from farm boy to master artist. Check out what he had to say about his journey.

Paul's Journey

BoP: You had a goal to become an incredible artist, and you wanted to paint like other people or better than other people. You had this journey that included not only your skills developing but also certain things about yourself that had to develop. Give me an illustration of something about you that had to change along your journey to reach the professionalism and master artistry you are capable of today?

PAJ: The very first step was to move away from the farm to break the glass of the fishbowl. Being contained on a farm with little or no inspiration, to gain any skill would be to travel, to move, to get out in the world, and see what's out there. To have other influences both in meeting personalities in who you look up to, which I did, and try to mimic the steps that they took.

Because of Purpose

Asking questions was also a really important step. **IT WAS GETTING THE RIGHT ANSWERS, WORKING ON THOSE ANSWERS, DEVELOPING THEM, PUTTING THEM TO THE TEST IN MANY AVENUES** in both painting and drawing. This was a huge influence. These things help me to get up that hill. I'm going to use a scenario of getting up a hill because there were those who pushed me from behind.

There were those who challenged me, those who encouraged me, and then the people ahead of me that were pulling me, meaning my customers. The people who were ahead of me were my customers. They would say to me, "Hey, Paul. I have this job. Can you do it?" That's like gaining some leverage to help you get up the mountain, so to speak.

I never said no. That's why my portfolio is filled with a variety of things because I never said no.

"Hey Paul, can you paint a raccoon?" Yes.

"Paul, can you paint a ship flying through the clouds?" Yes.

What they don't see is Paul Jones with his head in his hands at the table in front of the easel, going, "How am I going to do this?" I wanted the job, but I also wanted my portfolio full so that I can show people. "Look what I've done, look at what I can do."

So, it wasn't just me. Yes, it was me wanting that attitude of getting up there. **YOU ALWAYS HAVE TO HAVE THAT POSITIVE ATTITUDE GETTING UP THAT HILL.** But it takes people both pushing you and those who are encouraging you to get up that hill.

BoP: Today, your mental file cabinet is filled with, "Yes, I can figure this out."

Your history says, "Yes, I figured it out."

What about fifteen years ago, or twenty years ago, when you were presented with a new challenge? What things did you have to do to be able to move into a place where you could take on that new challenge, that new technique, that new concept or object?

PAJ: Scribbling, doodling, and plenty of research, always research. That is my map, if you will. Research equals a blueprint. Research forms that blueprint that you need, that guide.

If you're going to build a house, you drive around some roads looking at property first. Where are you going to put the house? Then you finally get that piece of property. You go through a realtor, and you get the price. Now you are looking at that road that goes by that property, and you go, "I want a house, but where am I going to put it?"

You start looking around the property and think, "Maybe over there. No, wait, maybe over there." Maybe get some input from your spouse or family. "Hey, guys. Where do you think the best location is for this house?" How far from the road? How tall? How big? That's the research aspect. That's the brainstorming.

That's the same as artwork. Where am I going to put this on the canvas? How will it be positioned? What light source am I going to use? What tones am I going to use?

Sometimes I will start out by scribbling out ideas. You don't ever take on a challenge, saying, "Oh, I'm going to do this," and then sit down at the canvas and start painting. That's not how it's done. It requires planning. **So, planning and research are always the tools that will get me through the challenge that I have not yet done.**

BoP: The painting that you did for me called Airship, the ship flying through the clouds, which is near and dear to my

Because of Purpose

heart. You have this gigantic tall ship that is shredding clouds, coming out of a cloud bank, blowing the clouds out, the sails are straining, and the whole ship is in the air. How much research and what type of research was necessary for you to be able to do that painting?

PAJ: Well, as you know, we started out with sketches. Remember, I did the one through five sketches? Then we tweaked as we went along. It was you, because of the way you look at things, that conceived of this concept.

I had no knowledge of nautical building or how things are put together in ships. I had to rely on your understanding of that. I also looked up ships online. As you know, we went through the whole thing with how is the mast assembled, how are the ship's sails sewn, how does a bow and bowsprit look? I researched all this.

BECAUSE THERE IS REALLY NO PAINTING OR A PICTURE TO GO BY, THIS WAS ALL FORMED, CONCEIVED, AND PUT TOGETHER BY PURE THOUGHT. Remember all the sketches we went through. You would say tilt it this angle or that way until we got it right. How low should the ship be compared to the viewpoint of the viewer? All of those things were taken into consideration with the simple pencil and paper sketch.

The amount of research that occurred before I actually laid any paint to the canvas at all, I would think about eight to nine hours. This was scribbling, going back to you with each new sketch, and then I made the stencil. I took a piece of poster board and actually constructed a stencil to use for position and alignment. So we're talking about nine hours total on that.

On the actual painting, it was over a span of twenty-seven days, so the hours that I actually worked on it, I think this one took fifty-one hours to paint. That is because of perspective. The angles that had to be just right; the lighting had to be just right; the impression of speed coming out of the clouds had to be just right.

BoP: OK. You get to the point that you are all done. You put your paints down, you clean off your brush, what is the feeling as you stand back and look at it as a completed work, you are waiting for it to dry so you can ship it? What is that feeling?

PAJ: The feeling is relief knowing that I have it done, but the feeling is mixed with, and I'm going to say this because I want to be perfectly honest with you, fear. Satisfied that I completed the physical task of putting the design onto a canvas, but fear that my customer will not accept it. My goal relies heavily on the satisfaction of the customer.

The painting I'm working on right now, for example, the customer does not want to see any progression pictures. She wants to see it in shock value, her words.

She said, "I know your work, I love your work, I know you're the best of the best, but I don't want you to show me one glimpse of it until you get it done." That, to me, is fearful. Here's why.

I have been the customer of people I wanted stuff done for me. I want to see it done in transition. I want to see how it's progressing along the way in case there's anything I want to change. When I am painting, I want total perfection.

So, to answer your question, yes, satisfied that I've done the job, thrilled that I've finally completed that piece, but now comes the approval process.

BoP: What would you say is the most outstanding painting that you've ever done? The one painting that absolutely filled you with the most joy when you were done with it?

PAJ: The Ascension. The reason why is that it had been thirty-four years, since I was sixteen, unknowledgeable, still living on a farm, old oil paint that I did not like, and it was a hot summer when I was painting it in June and July. But to have that remake, and to see the difference between sixteen and fifty, that was the crowning achievement. Not only was it a painting, but it was a large mural.

BoP: Every eleven years, you do a remake of a painting that you did when you were eleven, that really got you started. When you look back at your eleven-year-old rendition, what were the thoughts when you were painting that, about your future for painting?

PAJ: At that time, all of my siblings were painting, mainly from the influence of my dad, who was painting. He was a good artist, not refined, but good. Since dad did it, we all tried it. I was the one who wanted to take it further than dad, further than the artists I had already seen. It was just a personal thing. I felt that I wanted to do that even better.

I still know those emotions from the first time I sat and painted. I am fifty-four and a half, and I can still feel the same emotions. I was using dad's brushes and dad's paint and canvas. I felt lost. My sister, my late sister, who was also an artist, was somewhat guiding me through.

I remember painting the pine trees first, then the barn, and then I painted the sky. Total reverse order that it should have been in, but I didn't know. My goal was to paint something that I thought of and get it on to the canvas. That was my goal.

So, the emotions were a sense of being lost because I didn't know how to do it. A few tips from my dad and a few tips from my sister was all I had. Well, you got to start somewhere, right?

The second time I did it, I thought, "You know, that was eleven years ago. I think I'll do it again. Wow, what a difference.

Twenty-two years later, I look back at that second one and go, "What was I thinking?" And the third remake, of course, I was thirty-three years old, I did it better than the second, and I thought, "Wow! Why didn't I think of that eleven years ago."

When I was forty-four, I did the fourth rendition, and next year I will be fifty-five, so I will do it again February. When I look at the fourth one, I will think, "Really? I sold that to the public?" When I look at them and see what areas I fixed, it's so visible. We're talking about color, to perspective, to detail, to realism, to everything.

BoP: How long have you, if you have started yet, preparing for your fifty-five-year-old rendition?

PAJ: Six years now.

BoP: When you completed your forty-four-year rendition, were you wondering how much better your fifty-five-year rendition would be?

PAJ: As I was sitting there painting it, yes.

BoP: How do you approach that eleven-year-old rendition? Is there still pride in what you did?

PAJ: There is pride, yes, because I actually completed the painting. There is satisfaction in not doing it halfway, which some of my siblings did.

How I look at it today is how could I have not known that in my physical body, I can look at a scene similar to that but not paint it as it is. Then I begin to realize **IT'S NOT WHAT YOU SEE; IT'S HOW YOU SEE IT.**

I look at the fence post, and it's just one solid color. I know what it is, it's just that it didn't have any wood grain, it didn't have any bleaching from the sun or weathering. It was just a straight solid color.

BoP: So now that you've gotten the years of experience and the vast number of total success that you've had in your career, and now you see what you see differently, whereas before you didn't have the kind of knowledge or experience to understand what you saw back when you were eleven.

PAJ: Right. That scene came out of my head. I can't go back to the place and say, "Oh, there it is." It doesn't exist, so the details were lost.

BoP: So the visualization has gone to, "I've seen this in reality, so now I can bring it into a completely creative place where I can begin to do my own."

PAJ: Correct. You couldn't have said that any better if you tried. I'm going to fall back for a moment and take an exit here.

There was a painting I did called a group of memories. It is a fictitious river with a slight waterfall. One of my best paintings I did back at the time I did it, back about twenty-something years ago. I combined a lot of Southern Missouri scenes in my imagination, coming out of pure thought, and put them into one painting. That was the concept I had when I did my first one. Now that I'm about to redo it, I realize it's not what you see, but how much your imagination allows you to see in your mind's eye.

BoP: If you saw a painting that had the obvious technical skill but lacked the creativity, would you say that this person is not an experienced painter, or would you say that this person hasn't had enough life experience to be able to translate to the canvas well?

PAJ: The latter, definitely the latter. With experience comes creativity. Anybody can sit in a studio and copy a bluejay. There's a bluejay on a branch. So they replicate that and make a bluejay on a branch, but it's just a bluejay on a branch. There's no real interesting thing about it. It's just a bird sitting there, and that's about it. It's very generic.

Now, if you took that same bird, its wings are expanded, its claws are coming out, its mouth is open, in a striking position, and there's a black snake on that same branch getting ready to strike back at it, there's a fight going on, you've added drama. You've added something interesting, and the viewer can go, "Wow! That black snake thinks that branch is his." Or "That bluejay thinks the branch is his." The viewer's mind gets excited by filling in the gaps. It's still a picture that is perfectly held still. Only **THE EMOTIONS ARE NOW FULLY INVOLVED, SO THE MIND IS COMPLETELY ENGAGED.**

BoP: Thank you very much for your time, Paul. You have definitely given us a great picture of your journey, and you have shared with us a lot of wisdom that not only applies to painting and art but the road of success itself.

PAJ: Glad to help.

Thoughts

It was an absolute blast to spend some time with my friend, Paul.

At the beginning of the interview, Paul talked about getting the right answers and putting them into practice. We discussed this in chapter six. You need to be aware of the things you might need to learn, or seek help with, to be able to complete your plan.

Also, keeping a positive attitude is vital on your way to conquering your dreams. This does not mean you are supposed to be a happy go lucky person 24 by 7. That is an unrealistic expectation. What it does mean is as you run into issues, don't give up but keep pushing through. Look, study, read, research, think, ask people. Do whatever it takes to press past the issue, knowing that there is an answer, and it will come about.

Several times, Paul mentioned using pure thought to come up with the ideas that helped to create the next painting. Your mind is a powerful ally, and once you are more accustomed to using it in this way, you will be amazed at the things you can come up with.

As Paul was discussing the remaking of his eleven-year-old painting, I thought about the folks who try to compare their beginning to someone else's middle. Do what you are doing with the skills you have today. Don't worry about anyone else. Just make it happen. Sure, you might think that in five or ten years, this would be easier, or you would have more knowledge on the subject. That's true, but do not let that stop you today. Each time Paul paints the picture, it's about making that current one the best possible. He knows that in another eleven years, his skill will be better, but that doesn't stop him from completing it and doing the best possible.

We talked about having the emotions fully involved in a painting. Paul said that the whole mind will get behind it if the feelings are engaged. When you see your vision board with your dreams on it, when you read your goal description, as you are saying your affirmations each day, get your emotions busy. This will help activate your mind even more.

I hope you caught a few things about Paul's journey to being a Master Artist that you can apply to achieve your goals and dreams.

Chapter 11

The Beginning

In closing just sounds so permanent, like something is over, but it isn't. So I have called this section The Beginning.

In the pages of this book, I have shown you the beginning. The beginning of what? The beginning of whatever you want to do in your life.

You are free to invent your life.

- Fortune Cookie

Challenge yourself. Take bold steps and accomplish big things. This is what it is all about.

Purpose and Passion

There is something that I think is worth pointing out before you charge strong after your future, which is the right way to do it—just saying. I want to talk about what purpose is and how it differs from passion.

There is a concept that talks about having a direction in life. It is a Japanese word called ikigai, which means "a reason for being." Ikigai describes purpose, or what it calls your mission, like a cross between what you love and what the world needs. When you are in love with some idea or concept, and it serves to better you, those around you, or is something for the greater good, this is your purpose or mission.

For me, as you already know, it is teaching. It is something I love to do, and it is useful for those I can reach. The same thing goes for the other items on my attributes list. Affection is something I love, and my family feels my love toward them. Also, peace is one of my life attributes. If I can create an environment of peace, which I like to live in, then it makes me better able to respond to my loved ones, and it allows them to live in that same peaceful atmosphere.

The dictionary defines purpose as the reason something is done, the desired result, and fortitude. Your reason, your desired result, and your fortitude is the purpose. When you think back to Chapter Two, we talked about the trip of driving from Seattle to Miami. We knew that we needed a reason for making that long trip that was greater than the reason to stay put. Here is a quote from chapter two.

"One thing you are challenged with on this journey is establishing 'why.' If you are in Seattle and you want to get to Miami, it's always worth the time and the effort to ask yourself, why do you want to get to Miami? **The reason for the journey is the 'purpose of the trip'.***"*

Because of Purpose

Understanding your purpose can help you define your reason and the other way around. Understanding your reason will strengthen your purpose and your resolve. This is why getting emotionally connected with your goals and your reasons is so important.

Passion is a little different. According to ikigai, passion is also what you love, but it is combined with what you are good at, or can be good at one day. When you have something you love, and you are good at it, then you have a passion or a hunger for it.

I have a passion for sailing. There is just something special about pulling up the sails on a sailboat, and tuning them until the boat moves under the power of the wind alone. No other sound is heard, just the wind and the water on the hull. I enjoy it, and I'm a pretty decent sailor too.

Now, I wouldn't say that sailing a boat would do something for the world. It doesn't quite fit as a purpose in my case. I do have a goal to cruise around all of the islands in the Caribbean. The most number of people that it would benefit would be my wife and me. That's about it. It is not something that would benefit anyone more than the two of us. It matches my life attributes of adventure and freedom, so it is a goal that fits me perfectly, which is about completing the goal and enjoying my passion.

Sailing would not be a useful purpose for me, but there can be a purpose in the journey. As we meet people and can tell their stories to others upon our return, we might inspire someone to do something that will benefit people to a greater good. You never know what might happen in life when others can see that you did something extraordinary.

Faith is expecting the desired outcome, no matter what.

-Vann Lantz

Almost Never Wins

A book I read once told the story of a man who was allowed to meet some of the most remarkable people in history, learning a life lesson from each of them. The last one was an angel in a vast, unending warehouse full of things. The angel explains that this warehouse contains the goals that people had in their lives, but they gave up too soon. The angel explained it like this.

The tragedy of life is not that man loses, but that he almost wins.

- Andy Andrews

In marathons, some cross the finish line, and some don't. Those that finish are the ones with the grit, determination, and the will to win.

Unfortunately, winning in our society today means coming in first. This idea causes a lot of people who themselves might do great things, to never even try. If they can't come in first, why put in the effort? This thought process is, of course, ridiculous.

Yes, it feels great to win, but to all who cross the line, it means they have put in the work with training, they have been exercising, eating right, getting better equipment to run with, and a host of other things. Above all, they stayed with it until the end.

Please do not confuse this with a goal to win. If you are an athlete and want a gold medal around your neck, then your goal is to be first. But, if your goal is a dream vacation, starting a business, or learning a language, then the only thing that counts is to cross the finish line.

Get a good idea and stay with it. Dog it, and work at it until it's done, and done right.

- Walt Disney

Walt Disney built an empire. The theme parks and movies all bare his name. How did this happen? Because he started with a good idea. He stuck with it until it was done.

Recently I read a story about a man named Frank Gunsaulus. He was a preacher with a burning desire to create a higher education school where they taught not just theory but taught with their hands.

Because of Purpose

Gunsaulus figured it would take one million dollars to start this school. Back in 1890, that was a ton of cash. For two years, he thought about ways to get the money to open the school. He preached one morning a sermon about what he would do if he had a million dollars. Unbeknownst to Gunsaulus, in the audience that day, was a man named Philip Amour, a wealthy man in the meat industry. After hearing the sermon, Amour agreed to fund the school that Gunsaulus wanted to start.

That idea brought forth a school that is today called the Illinois Institute of Technology. It has been successful and growing since it opened in 1893. Gunsaulus had a vision, and he dogged it until he got the funds to start the school and then served as the president for many years.

You see, you must finish. You don't have to be the fastest to your goal, or the richest one to cross the line, or anything else other than someone who finished!

As we close our time together, I want to leave you with a powerful quote taken from the movie Tomorrowland. The bad guy, the mayor David Nix of Tomorrowland, was about to 'off' the heroes. As most bad guys will do, he gave a speech, which perfectly captured a growing problem for today. Most people, knowing that their situation will not get any better without doing something about it, still don't do anything about it. Why? Because the not-so-great future that they have resigned themselves to doesn't require from them any additional effort or action.

If you glimpsed the future and were frightened by what you saw, what would you do? ... In every moment, there is the possibility of a better future, but you people won't believe it. Because you won't believe it, you won't do what is necessary to make it a reality. So you dwell on the terrible future, and you resign yourself to it for one reason, because that future doesn't ask anything of you today.

- Mayor David Nix – Tomorrowland

Do not give up your dreams!

www.ingramcontent.com/pod-product-compliance
Lightning Source LLC
LaVergne TN
LVHW051459070426
835507LV00022B/2843